Also by Mark Kimmel

Trillion

Decimal

One

Icebreakers

Transformation

Birthing a New Civilization

Chrysalis

Cosmic Paradigm

Aon

Voices of the Nonphysicals

To Cheyenne Bart
Join us to create a new world
Mark Kimmel

Mark Kimmel

AON
Voices of the Nonphysicals

Mark Kimmel

FIRST EDITION

Paradigm Books
PO Box 538
Arroyo Grande, California 93421
cp@zqyx.org

www.cosmicparadigm.com

ISBN 9781688029507

Printed in the United States of America

This book is dedicated to the Great Beings of Light
whose words fill the following pages.

Several of the Great Beings of Light featured in this book have NOT made their existence known before. I believe you will find each of them to be unique. Their messages are most easily understood when read in the order presented.

Lord Metatron

Zi-An

Actin

Adama

Adrial and Justine

Es-Su and Alici

An-Ra-Ta

Ea-Ta

Aon

Yeshua

Mary of Bethany

Master Kuthumi

Archangel Michael

Lord Metatron

Lord Metatron

I am Lord Metatron, the Overseer of the transformation of all physical realms of this universe. I come to you this day to introduce you to this important book and to encourage you to read all facets of it. Each word in this text is accompanied by energies that will be imparted to you as you read. They are our gift to you. I leave it to each one who reads the words in this book to determine how it affects them individually.

I will now touch on several points contained in the following pages. Those who are communicating hereafter will elaborate on them. We are revealing to you, the humans of Earth, certain details of the universe in which you live, so that you may see beyond the confines of the conventional paradigm of Earth and thereby raise your consciousness to positively affect all.

This book will reveal much about the creation and operation of the universe, Earth, and her physical beings. It will give insights into Great Non-physical Beings and non-humans, both here on Earth and those who occupy other planets, star systems and galaxies.

Our intent is to supply you with information to assist you to understand why you are here at this time and what you can do to make the best use of your time while in this life.

✳✳✳✳✳✳✳✳✳✳

At the beginning of this universe, our Collective of Great Overseers set out to implement the Schematic of Source, a living blueprint of what Source desired all in the universe to become. It was understood that nothing would be created without a path to achieve this goal. Another name for this goal is Christ Consciousness.

Lord Metatron

With this directive, we expressed Creator Gods to undertake the creation of the initial galaxies, stars, planets, and physical beings. We also manifested Oversouls who would supply the souls for them. While creations within this Schematic would be individual, all would operate as members of collectives.

The first galaxies were created with mixed energies or consciousness. Stars were created as part of these first galaxies. Some stars spun off planets as homes for physical beings; some did not. All physical beings on a planet had a similar goal: To raise the energy of all by raising the energy of the individual.

A few billion years later, there were galaxies, stars, planets, and physical beings on paths that would lead to high consciousness. The Milky Way Galaxy was one of these.

Based on observations and speculations of scientists operating from a 3rd Dimension point of view, and others who base their views on various beliefs, there are many theories about the creation of the universe. The reality is that the universe began as the cooperative effort of Overseers such as myself along with Creator Gods and Oversouls who functioned based on the Schematic of Source. It took millions of years to organize and billions of years to implement. Chance and chaos were never involved.

As this great undertaking progressed, we expressed additional Creator Gods to create galaxies, stars, planets, and physical beings. We also manifested additional Oversouls to supply the souls for each of these creations.

We created a collective of Unique Oversouls that would incarnate very high consciousness souls into high-energy physical beings to create Avatars and other highly conscious physical beings. These would illustrate their consciousness by living and teaching Christ Energy.

Lord Metatron

At the onset of the creation of this universe, my collective also created a number of very special planets that would model the Schematic of Source by their perfection of Light, Love, and Unity within the physical environment and within the lives of the physical beings who would inhabit them. Earth was one of these.

From the very beginning we foresaw that there was enough flexibility in the overall grand plan for the universe that things might vary from the Schematic of Source, before returning to it. All went according to plan with the creation and functioning of the Creator Gods, Oversouls, galaxies, stars, planets, and physical beings.

Source expressed Archangels to assist us in monitoring the activities of the universe, to assist Creator Gods and Oversouls, and to assist individual planets and physical beings. Legions of angels were created with the charge of assisting individual physical beings.

My Collective of Overseers created Earth as a special planet. It was to act as a model of Christ Consciousness for the Milky Way Galaxy, to illustrate the perfection of the Schematic of Source. Earth was placed above the plane of the Milky Way Galaxy in order to show its perfection to all planets of the Galaxy. This time of modeling, known as Earth's Golden Era, continued for a billion years.

After the Milky Way Galaxy had stabilized itself, there were Creator Gods that wished to experiment with integrating dense matter and higher energies. These experiments, which took place outside the Schematic of Source, went on for some time. Some were marginally successful, most were not. Entire planets were destroyed as not viable.

Lord Metatron

From these experiments a dark energy emerged. It was based on denying the dependence of all on Source. Like a cancer, this dark energy infected individual physical beings and entire planets. Such experiments with integrating dense matter and higher energies were conducted on Earth. These eventually led to the near-destruction of Earth, the beacon of the Milky Way Galaxy. This event is known as the Great Catastrophe.

Before Earth could be returned to Source for re-creation as a special planet of Light, we determined to restart it as a 3rd Dimension planet and set a goal for it to ascend to 12th Dimension. This planetary resurrection has been on-going for several billion years. Each human of Earth is charged with assisting the planet to achieve its goal as a 12th Dimension planet.

The dark energy that resulted from the experiments on Earth during its Golden Era carried over to the new Earth of 3rd Dimension. It infects many on Earth today, causing them to act from fear, anger, judgment, and domination, and to seek power and wealth.

There have been many Avatars who have lived on Earth according to Christ Consciousness, even though they may not have been recognized as such. Some of these will speak in the following chapters.

This book will detail what I have spoken of and will assist you to understand why you incarnated on Earth: You are a special physical being on a sacred mission. There are many Great Beings of Light who support you as you live on Earth at this moment.

Blessings,
Metatron

Zi-An

Zi-An

Zi-An

I am Zi-An , one of the Creator Gods of the Collective of Galactic Creator Gods who created the Milky Way Galaxy. In perfect alignment with the Schematic of Source, we created the billions of stars and planets in this Galaxy.

At the direction of Source, Galactic Creator Gods created all the galaxies of this universe. Although we possess no physical form, we control the vast energies used to create the stars and planets of galaxies. If it were possible to count beings like us in the universe, we would number many billions for there are millions of galaxies and each galaxy has billions of stars.

There are two different Collectives of Creator Gods. Collectives of Galactic Creator Gods like mine create galaxies, stars, and planets. Planetary Creator Gods sculpt and nurture the physical forms of individual planets and create physical beings.

✶✶✶✶✶✶✶✶✶✶

When Source, operating through the Great Overseers of the Universe, determines that a galaxy is to be formed, a Collective of Galactic Creator Gods is expressed. In some cases, Galactic Creator Gods may transfer from a completed galaxy where they have gained valuable experiences. In the early moments of creation, when we created galaxies like the Milky Way, we did not have Creator Gods with billions of years of experience. Nonetheless, the process is essentially the same. It always involves a Collective of Galactic Creator Gods with the requisite powers. There are specific directives for each galaxy within the grand plan of the Schematic of Source.

Zi-An

The undirected Light of Source is everywhere throughout this universe. As the basic building block of All That Is, it is available to be transformed into physical form. We access this Light in the area in which we are directed to create a galaxy, then we activate the energy of Love to form our creation. Light is the material; Love is the energy. We transform undirected Light into light with purpose.

In the beginning of an intended galaxy there is no form, no color, and no sound. Our Collective first converts undirected Light into form as an irregular mass of gases. This irregular form is many lightyears in diameter, much larger than the galaxy into which it will be condensed.

This initial step requires more than a billion years of linear time, were we to measure time in that way. At the completion of this event, time and space begins for a galaxy.

The next step is to create a central core and give it rotation. The central core is where physical mass is concentrated and where individual stars are born. It is a place where gaseous form is concentrated into enough density to be called physical. Individual stars are thrust from the core in such a way as to align with the intended rotation of the galaxy.

These birthing stars are seldom perfect globes, so each is carefully attended by a Galactic Creator God to insure its final shape and size. Each is molded in anticipation of the planets it will later spin off and the physical beings thereon. Each star is then guided to its position within the galaxy, be it close to the core or on a spiral arm distant from the core.

To call the powerful energy core of a galaxy a "black hole" does this magnificent process an injustice as well as ignoring the creative participation of Galactic Creator Gods. What scientists see as a well into which stars are drawn is really the generator from which stars are thrust outward. They speculate it as a very dense place without light; it is in reality a place of extraordinary energy that gives birth to individual stars.

The process we Creator Gods use to create a galaxy and star

systems is not unlike what your astronomers theorize. However, humans of lower consciousness are unable to see the very active guidance that Galactic Creator Gods carry out during the process of creation. At some future time, scientists of Earth will come to accept our involvement. For now, it is my task to lay it out for those who would accept my words.

✶✶✶✶✶✶✶✶✶✶

Each star emerges at an extremely high temperature; they subsequently cool as they prepare to spin-off planets. Then a decision is made as to what type planets this newly created sun is to spin off, gaseous or solid, large or small. This results in the formation of physical elements within the star. This, in turn, determines the various physical elements that will be imparted to the planets of a star, which then result in atmosphere, solid mass, and water.

All of this is carefully geared to the type of physical beings who will eventually inhabit the planets of a star. It requires billions of years to generate the billions of individual stars of a galaxy, and many more to create planets. Each star receives a soul expressed from one of the Galactic Oversouls of the Milky Way Galaxy.

Each star is a transformer of energies. It will subsequently receive energies from the core of the Galaxy and radiate them to the surrounding planets. Each is a globe of plasma; they are not the nucleus of an atomic reaction. Each star receives energies from the core of the galaxy to sustain its power. In turn they transform these energies and radiate them to the planets in orbit, including different wave lengths of light and energy. These energies are essential for the plants, animals, and physical beings of a planet.

The next step is to create planets around individual stars and the process is somewhat reversed. Here the stars are initially denser than the proposed individual planets. After we give stars rotation, gaseous material is ejected from them. Under our guidance this material is then formed into various individual planets, each a unique combination of physical elements.

I was delighted to see the gaseous forms of planets emerge from a star that I had created. We formed each planet into a unique sphere with the beginnings of a unique environment, be it solid, liquid, gaseous, or combinations thereof. Basic rock formations, water, and atmosphere resulted from this process. Few of the planets of the Milky Way Galaxy resemble your current Earth, yet they are ideal for sustaining their own physical life forms. Each planet receives a planetary soul from a Galactic Oversoul.

As we complete the formation of the planets of a galaxy, we hand them off to a Collective of Planetary Creator Gods. They then assume control of the planets, guide their evolution, and create physical beings.

They both direct and utilize evolution to manage the formation of the planet and the seeding and progress of plants, animals and physical beings over the ensuing billions of years. What your scientists attribute to some sort of natural evolution is, in reality, the guidance of Planetary Creator Gods.

Like a concerned parent, over the next billion years I watched as the Planetary Creator Gods prepared the planets of this galaxy for their intended use as playgrounds for physical beings. From time to time, I visited planetary creations to view the plants, animals, and physical beings that the Planetary Creator Gods had created or imported from other planets. I enjoyed seeing the beings of form for each planet with the souls supplied by Planetary Oversouls.

The vastness and beauty of the Milky Way Galaxy is indeed wondrous to behold. Those of us involved in its creation are well aware of how well it functions according to the Love and Unity of the Schematic of Source, what you term Christ Consciousness.

You might relate it to a symphony orchestra with each instrument playing its part to create beautiful music.

In contrast to the other planets of the Milky Way Galaxy, Earth is unique. Great Beings of Light, closely associated with Source, created Earth's physical form. It did not go through the more usual creation by Galactic Creator Gods as part of a star system. It was formed directly from the Light of Source.

They created Earth to be a magnificent sphere, a perfect example of the living Schematic of Source. This took place as the Milky Way Galaxy was just in its initial formation under the guidance of Galactic Creator Gods. These Great Beings of Light positioned Earth above the plane of the Milky Way Galaxy so that her radiation of Christ Consciousness could affect all other planets of the Galaxy. As the stars of the Milky Way Galaxy were created and began slowly rotating about its core, Earth stood apart from that rotation.

As Earth formed into its initial shape and density, atmosphere, land, and water were separated. Then followed a period as the planet was prepared to receive her inhabitants. When the energy of Earth stabilized at 12th Dimension, highly conscious beings of semi-physical form were created by Great Beings of Light.

This period of Earth's history is called her "Golden Era." It continued for billions of years, until her high energy was lost due to the Great Catastrophe. After the time of dormancy, I was one of the Creator Gods who inserted Earth's dense sphere of 3rd Dimension into its current orbit about your sun.

During the long-ago time of Earth's Golden Era, your planet stood out among all other planets, giving a powerful indication of the beauty of Christ Consciousness for all in the Galaxy. If you had seen it at that time, you would have called it a star. The inhabitants of Earth star were at 12th Dimension. The inhabitants of many other planets patterned themselves after its example of living in accord with the Schematic of Source. Individual beings from these planets visited Earth to absorb its beauty and to see an example of the way in which Source intended all to be.

✶✶✶✶✶✶✶✶✶✶

After the creation of the Milky Way Galaxy, and during the time Earth and her inhabitants were enjoying her Golden Era and broadcasting Christ Energy to all in the Galaxy, experiments began on planets in one sector of the Galaxy. These experiments involved combining dense matter with higher dimensions. The beings involved believed their creations could function without the Light of Source. Along with a few Planetary Creator Gods they pursued the experiments because they saw a way to create something exciting, something that they had not encountered before. They became very committed to seeing the results of their creations.

Some resulting mis-creations, including entire planets, were destroyed as not viable. There were occasional results of the experiments that looked promising, so they were allowed to survive. The energies of these physical beings were sufficient so that after a while they began to reproduce. All of them had only a minimal Light of Source within, just enough to function at 3rd and 4th Dimensions.

Those beings who were pioneering the experiments did not realize, until it was too late, that dark energy, like a cancer, was being produced within the experiments. And like cancer, this dark energy infected them too, convincing them to continue with the experiments at all costs. As with many cancers, it infects the host without being observed until it is well advanced. Dark energy has many of the same characteristics of cancer as experienced in physical bodies. In fact, many cancers in physical bodies are caused by non-physical dark energy.

Zi-An

Souls expressed by Planetary Oversouls refused to incarnate in the mis-creations. At the same time, the resulting physical beings were intelligent and eventually learned to travel beyond their home planet. Realizing the limitations of physical bodies without souls, they set out to conquer other planets to mate with their physical beings in order to acquire higher functioning progeny.

When they conquered other planets, they did not necessarily use a forceful approach, rather they came as friendly beings who brought technology. In many cases they were welcomed and integrated into the population of a planet, as ones who would upgrade the functioning of the indigenous people.

From the very beginning, the beings that had been invaded by the dark energies had their eye on Earth because it was such a unique planet. They wished to be known as the ones who conquered it.

Invasive dark energies were brought to Earth by visitors from other planets. Some came to Earth from worlds with different atmospheres, so they had to adapt to Earth's atmosphere and could not remain long. The visitors portrayed themselves as benevolent even though they came from planets whose beings had been invaded by the dark energies of fear, separation, and domination. In the initial instances of this, the high consciousness beings of Earth were not affected by the dark energies associated with the visitors.

During these billions of years, inhabitants of the coherent planets that adhered to the Schematic of Source advanced into higher consciousness. They learned to travel beyond their own planets, but did not conquer other worlds. There was some peaceful migration to other planets where their high consciousness was welcomed.

As these events were playing out, a "war" developed between coherent planets that adhered to the Schematic of Source, versus planets that had been infected by the dark energies of fear and domination. Planets of high consciousness defended themselves against intrusions of dark beings by maintaining their high consciousness. This war has gone on for billions of years in this sector of the Milky Way Galaxy.

I observe that interactions between humans of Earth and beings from planets where dark energy has successfully invaded has continued to this day. In many cases the power of dark energy has been grossly distorted as overpowering. This is done by those aligned with it in order to incite fear and helplessness.

Despite publicity to the contrary, almost all planets of the Milky Way Galaxy, including this sector, are of higher consciousness. In the entire universe, less than one tenth of one percent of physical beings even know about the existence of lower dimensions such as represented by 3rd Dimension Earth.

I trust by now you understand just how vast the Milky Way Galaxy is. I also trust you understand the role that Creator Gods like myself played in its creation, all the way down to individual planets. And I trust that you see how special is Earth. From this I trust that you glimpse how special are you.

I am most pleased to present this information. May it enrich your life.

Blessings,
Zi-An

Mark Kimmel: On the following pages, I present my comments on Zi-An's communication. Comments at the end of subsequent chapters will be designated as **MK:** to distinguish them from the preceding communications.

The words on the prior pages were transcribed in close cooperation with Zi-An, a Great Being of Light. This revelation and those that follow impact us in many ways, giving us a greater knowledge of the wondrous universe in which we live, our role in it, and what we can do to give more meaning to our lives.

In my comments I sometimes use either "he" or "she" when referring to a Great Being of Light. However, they are nonphysical, so they have no gender. I have felt their energies as either masculine or feminine so have used that designation.

Some of this information has never before been available. At the very least, it will change your concept of God, the creation of the universe, and who you are. I am honored to be the scribe for these important messages.

✶✶✶✶✶✶✶✶✶✶

It is with Love and appreciation that I received Zi-An's communication. The words have given me new appreciation for the vastness and complexity of the universe in which I live. It has shown me the billion planets of the Milky Way Galaxy and the intense involvement of high consciousness non-physical beings with them. All this has given me an appreciation of just how special is the planet upon which I currently live.

As I learn more about the vastness of a galaxy such as the Milky Way, the creation of stars and planets, I am truly amazed. I have also learned that I have had many lives in which I explored this vastness. I am overwhelmed by all of it.

I now have a clearer understanding of Christ Consciousness as a universe norm along with the Schematic of Source. Both are living, dynamic blueprints of the way in which Source would have all in the universe of physical form live. Along with Love they form a dynamic for creation and evolvement that has been given to Overseers, Creator Gods, and Oversouls. We, the physical beings of this universe, have been created to fulfill this grand vision of Source.

I saw a new way to understand the energy of Love when Zi-An pointed out that it was essential to creations by the Galactic Creator Gods. Now Love is much more than a feeling between humans. It is essential for the creation of the universe. Perhaps the next time you tell your pet that you love it, you will think of the larger role of Love as an essential ingredient in this vast creation.

In 1988, I came upon information that led me to understand that Earth was not the only inhabited planet. Prior to that time, I believed that stories about people on other planets were science fiction and extraterrestrials were evil, and to be feared.

For the last thirty years, I have sought to learn more about the universe and other planets. I discovered the gap that scientists cannot explain between the mass of the universe and the calculated mass of all galaxies and stars. I now see it as the Light of Source available to be used to create in physical form.

Looking at the night sky and reading about the vastness of the universe has been astonishing for me since I was a young child camping out in the Rocky Mountains. Now with the insights provided by Zi-An, I have come to understand the vastness of physical creation, for it is indeed vast!

Scientists tell us the Milky Way galaxy is 90,000 light years in diameter. That's a lot of miles. Then I think of Earth and the distances and time it takes to travel to other continents. This is tiny compared to the distance to another planet in our solar system, let alone the distance to another star system. The vastness of the universe is truly beyond my comprehension.

Zi-An's information about Earth as a very special planet solves for me one question and raises many more about our place in the universe. Little did I know that at one time, long ago, Earth was the premier planet in this galaxy. This is such a contrast with the beliefs about other planets that scientists use to search the universe for signs of life similar to Earth's.

I have seen evidence of off-planet visitors, and know they were real. That beings from planets with dark energies are visiting Earth is not a surprise, as I had learned about this from other sources. How dark energy invaded their physical forms as a cancer is new information.

The information about the development of dark planets was most welcome as it contradicted other information that speaks to the overwhelming power of dark extraterrestrials. I now see how raising the consciousness of humans on this planet will positively affect all in this sector of the Galaxy, including planets where dark energy dominates.

I also note that there is no mention of fallen angels, unless one wants to consider the Creator Gods who undertook experiments to be them. While they violated the Schematic of Source in their experiments, it certainly could not be considered a Lucifer rebellion against God.

I now view dark energies as a cancer. I have seen them invade the psyche of a person, leading to fear, separation, and anger. I believe these same energies can invade the physical body of a person leading to various types of cancer. I see those who undertook the experiments as extremely curious to discover a new kind of physical being, nothing more.

I now see Source as vast non-form spirit occupying the entirety of our universe. I see the Schematic of Source as a dynamic blueprint that is growing in scope and function as creation seeks to attain all that Source envisions. The birth and death of stars gives testimony to this. It also speaks to the immortality of our souls as we move from one incarnation to the next, from one planet to the next, in an ever-growing ascension to eventually return to Source.

I have had many experiences using energy to heal physical

bodies, my own and others. I have witnessed and experienced the positive effects of body workers as well as programs such as Matrix Energetics, Organ and Cell Regeneration, and Energetic Matrix. Understanding how non-physical energies can positively affect the body, shows me how non-physical dark energies can, like a cancer, invade a human body causing disease. The conclusion that I draw from this is that, by holding positive non-physical energies within ourselves, we can prevent and heal many physical problems.

I am most honored to be communicating with a Great Being of Light who has created planets, stars, and galaxies, and who is committed to the Schematic of Source in his creations, to Christ Consciousness. Zi-An is a wonderful, powerful being. I am both honored and humbled. At this moment I am at a loss for words to explain how I feel. I do know that I am very grateful.

I believe that life is meaningless without the larger picture. I hope this communication from Zi-An assisted you to discover a new meaning for your life.

Thank you, Zi-An, for helping me see the larger picture.

Blessings,
Mark

Questions about Zi-An's communication:

- What influences did Zi-An assert during the creation of the Milky Way Galaxy?

- Who created 12th Dimension Earth and her first inhabitants?

- Where was Earth originally positioned in the Galaxy?

- How do Zi-An's revelations affect your life?

Actin

Actin

Actin

I am **Actin,** of the Collective of Planetary Creator Gods who constructed Earth after her initial creation by the Great Overseers of the universe and thereafter created the physical beings who now inhabit her.

At the time my Collective received Earth from her Overseer creators, she was a fully-formed globe of light so bright that she could have been easily mistaken for a star. She displayed beautiful colors of every imaginable hue and broadcast sounds of many tones.

Positioned above the plane of the Milky Way Galaxy, Earth stood alone as the stars and planets of the Galaxy were created and rotated about its center. Earth was unique among planets of the Milky Way Galaxy in that she had been fully formed at a very high dimension as the perfect reflection of the Schematic of Source. At her core was a matrix of Christ Energy.

The many planets that orbited the brilliant stars of the Milky Way Galaxy were created by Galactic Creator Gods, as previously explained by Zi-An.

After a billion years of our nurturing, Earth stabilized at 12th Dimension. Rock, atmosphere, and waters were formed by my Collective as we further condensed the gases of the original planet. During the next billion years, a beautiful garden-like environment emerged in keeping with Earth's high energy. Thus, began her Golden Era.

The Great Overseers of the universe then created adult 12th Dimension beings to populate Earth. Their Christ Conscious souls were manifested by the Overseers of the universe who then turned over further interactions with them to newly created Planetary Oversouls.

In the beginning there were only a few of these wonderful

Actin

Adam Kadman beings, but over many years they multiplied into· a million. Their progeny likewise received Christ Conscious souls at the time of their births. The beings of Earth's Golden Era would be considered semi-physical compared to the current density of humans.

There were male and female physical beings; however, they did not engage in sex as you know it. Rather, by using Light energy a new physical being was born. These children were able to absorb the behaviors and knowledge of their adult parents in a very short time.

Hereafter, when we use the word time, we refer to linear time such as you have in your 3rd Dimension. Time at the higher dimensions is simultaneous; all is now. There are, however, sequences of events. So, to be precise, the children absorbed the behaviors and knowledge of their parents in a relatively easy sequence of events.

We remained close to Earth over the billions of years of her Golden Age. We witnessed the establishment and flourishing of Lemuria. This civilization in different forms and at different dimensions occupied a large area on one side of the planet.

Many came from distant planets of the Milky Way Galaxy to witness the unique culture of Lemuria and to learn what it was like to live in perfect Christ Consciousness. During this period, Mark, I helped to create the physical form of your first incarnation via a light induced pregnancy. I followed you for several lifetimes thereafter as you enjoyed the splendor of the most unique planet in the Milky Way Galaxy.

✱✱✱✱✱✱✱✱✱✱

Some of the following was previously communicated by Zi-An, but our perspective as Planetary Creator Gods is somewhat different from him as a Galactic Creator God.

On other planets of the Milky Way Galaxy, during Earth's Golden Era, Planetary Creator Gods and physical beings were experimenting with trying to combine dense matter and higher energies. They were very excited at the prospect of creating new life forms even though these life forms were a deviation from the Schematic of Source. Some of these mis-creations resulted in grotesque beings who were not viable. These were destroyed, along with the planets whereon they lived. Other life forms showed promise so they were set aside. The mis-creation activities produced a variety of physical beings, not all of whom were humanoid.

One of the planets on which extensive experiments had been undertaken was named Atlantis. The experiments there had so affected the planet that it was headed for self-destruction. Desperate to continue their race, the beings of Atlantis searched for another planet where they could re-settle. Earth's exalted status made her a most desirable target.

The Atlantians petitioned the Lemurians to allow them to settle on Earth. This group of beings was not of the same 12th Dimension consciousness as were the Lemurians, but they had a relatively high consciousness and had physical forms compatible with the Lemurians. If accepted, the Atlantians promised to abandon their experiments.

Believing that their high consciousness would overwhelm any residual negative impact from Atlantian experiments, the Lemurians welcomed them to Earth. For the next million years the former Atlantians and the Lemurians lived compatibly at higher dimensions.

Meanwhile, the experiments continued on other planets of the Milky Way Galaxy. Beings from those planets visited Earth. Some of the dark energies from visitors of these planets remained on Earth. Memories were stirred in the former Atlantians who retained imprints of the experiments on their former planet.

A few Creator Gods of my Collective along with some of the beings of Lemuria began to experiment with combining dense matter and higher densities. I did not participate, nor did most of the Planetary Creator Gods and the beings of Lemuria.

Actin

The attraction of the experiments was the prospect of creating a new species of physical beings. Some of the experiments were somewhat successful; some were not. The majority of Lemurians objected to the experiments, so those who wished to continue were asked to leave Lemuria. They relocated to the other side of the planet, naming their new home Atlantis.

These relocated Atlantians saw Earth as a special planet among all others in the Milky Way Galaxy. Their argument was that, if a new type of being could be perfected on Earth, it would serve as a model for many other planets. Thus, there was great intensity among the participants. The experiments went on for thousands of years. During this period many in Atlantis became disenchanted with the experiments and distanced themselves from them.

After some time, the energies of the experiments in Atlantis began to affect the entire planet causing earthquakes and volcanos. Earth fell to lower densities. I petitioned the Planetary Creator Gods who were involved in the experiments to withdraw their support. Some heeded my contention that the experiments were against the Schematic of Source, some did not. Many beings of Atlantis stopped supporting the experiments. Nonetheless, the experiments continued.

Unwilling to risk contamination, some higher dimension beings left Earth. For the next thousand years the experiments continued while the frequency of the planet cycled between 10th Dimension and 12th Dimension.

At the same time, experiments continued on other planets of the Galaxy. Some of the experiments produced entire planets with very low consciousness. Many experiments were terminated. Worlds were destroyed. Many in my Collective of Earth's Planetary Creator Gods foresaw disaster and spoke to the Collectives of the other planets about the dangers of continuing.

Eventually the vibration of Earth fell to the 9th Dimension. It was now very difficult for someone like you, Mark, to live during these times. Your soul departed the planet, returning to the comfort of your Oversoul. Among those who remained, there was uncertainty as to the eventual outcome of the experiments, and indeed the future of the planet.

Nonetheless, the experiments continued with only marginal results; Earth fell to the 8th Dimension. With the frequency of the planet at such a low level, and with little hope of recovery, the great Christ Consciousness Energy that resided at the center of Earth was removed.

This left the planet floundering. The beings of Lemuria were unable to hold their higher consciousness. Their entire civilization disappeared beneath the surface of the ocean. Souls of the Lemurians returned to their Oversouls for rest and recovery after such difficult experiences.

Atlantis was left on its own. A majority of its residents now wished to terminate the experiments. However, those who were leading the projects won the argument, contending that the only way to return Earth to its former brilliance was to find a way to complete the experiments successfully.

Seeing this, some in Atlantis sought to preserve what had once been a great civilization. They gave some of the most important technologies, discoveries, and energies to benevolent beings of other star systems and galaxies. Some were placed deep within the Earth in an attempt to preserve the better aspects of Atlantian civilization.

All physical beings remaining on the planet perished in the final days as the entire civilization of Atlantis sunk into the depths of the planet. Their souls returned to their Planetary Oversouls. This failure of the premier planet of the Galaxy is known throughout the universe as the Great Catastrophe.

✶✶✶✶✶✶✶✶✶✶

It was apparent to all in my Collective of Planetary Creator Gods that Earth was headed for complete self-destruction. Collectively we agreed, along with the Archangels and the Universe Overseers, to freeze the planet in a state of suspended animation. There Earth was to remain until its fate could be determined. With no short-term resolution in sight, my Collective of Planetary Creator Gods was directed to other planets of the universe.

It was difficult for those of us who had created the original beings of Earth, and the magnificent planet upon which they had lived, to watch it all end. But we had no choice but to stand aside and watch as the planet was readied to be returned to Source for re-creation as a new Christed Planet of Light. At that moment, the failure of the planet was very real.

After 500 million years of dormancy and much deliberation among Great Beings of Light, it was determined that Earth would be restarted as a 3rd Dimension planet with an objective of restoring it to the 12th Dimension. The Galactic Creator Gods moved the planet into an orbit around your sun where there had been no planet before. This required stabilizing Earth in her new orbit, stabilizing the rotation of the planet, and fixing her rotation by re-orienting her poles. The Galactic Creator Gods also stabilized the orbits of adjacent planets due to the influence of their new neighbor.

My Collective of Planetary Creator Gods, who had been busy on other planets, was summoned back to assist in the re-creation of the new Earth, as a starting point for its evolution to higher consciousness. Our first task was to take the great mass of rocks and waters of a lifeless sphere and begin to create tiny life forms that would lead to plants and larger life forms.

✷✷✷✷✷✷✷✷✷✷

Actin

The guided evolution of Earth from rocks and waters to a sphere suitable for human beings took several billion years through many stages of carefully guided evolution. For the first billions of years, there was only the interplay between the waters, the atmosphere, and the rocks, as we carved out mountains and oceans. We recognized that Earth possessed unique natural resources as a special planet of Light. We laid plans to utilize this uniqueness in order to create a truly beautiful environment for humanity.

I recall how I enjoyed repeatedly guiding waters through rock layers to form what you now call the Grand Canyon. Others of my Collective enjoyed moving the crust of the planet to form the great mountains of Tibet, and the repeated uplifting and volcanic activity required to form mountain ranges like the Rockies and Alps. Using our foresight, we designated areas to evolve into prairie, wooded terrain, or desert, areas with rivers or lakes, and areas of higher plateaus or lower elevations. Billions of years passed as Earth's surface underwent change after change due to the rising and subsiding of land, plus the incursions and withdrawals of oceans.

We guided Earth through these various stages of maturing. Then we created plant life that started small, and under our guidance, evolved into trees and sources of nourishment for forthcoming animals. In the oceans, we established a great diversity of plant life that would later nourish the creatures of the seas. There was an age of dinosaurs, as we matured Earth's land, waters, and atmosphere.

About one billion years ago, when all was finally stabilized and lush, we introduced a great variety of animals, birds, fish, and insects. Some we created unique to Earth. Some were brought from other planets. All lived in harmony with Earth's environment.

Each species of animal, insect, bird, fish, or reptile had a function within the overall environment of Earth. From the smallest spider to the largest cockroach, from the squirrel to the elephant, and from the hummingbird to the eagle, each has a role in the health of the planet.

Each blade of grass, each bush, and each tree, each flower, berry, and fruit, all are part of the overall plan of my Collective.

Actin

After their initial creation, each species was allowed to develop. We used carefully guided evolution to create what you have today.

All the while we were focused on developing a world suitable for the introduction of humanity. We had been directed to bring this 3rd Dimension planet to a place with easily available necessities for human life. The end result of our efforts was a veritable paradise for early humans. With little effort, they could find sufficient food, water, and shelter to sustain themselves. Imprints of this are what gave rise to the story of the Garden of Eden.

During these billions of years, we installed the basic laws of mathematics, physics, chemistry, and biology. It would be a mistake to assume that these laws are the same on other planets of the universe. They are not.

✳✳✳✳✳✳✳✳✳✳

500,000 years ago, we created a group of humanity's original ancestors. These first adults were very primitive. Our original creations were not related to other physical beings in the universe, nor were they related to the animals of Earth.

They possessed just enough intelligence and physical skills for survival. Their souls were not integrated into their bodies, they had minimal intelligence, and their sole focus was on surviving. We gave them a rational mind so they could analyze their circumstances and make decisions about other physical beings, about staying safe, finding food, and water. To assist humanity in navigating 3rd Dimension we provided linear time to their rational minds.

Only a single species of humanoids was created so we might observe their survival and propagation in Earth's 3rd Dimension environment. They possessed a sex drive to begin the propagation of the race. The development of these early ancestors of modern humans advanced very slowly. Our main objective was to create a species that would evolve to 12th Dimension.

Actin

Testing the limits of their physical bodies, and despite what had been provided for them in the way of food, they learned to kill and eat animals and birds. It was more than a hundred thousand years before humans discovered fire. This all took place over hundreds of thousands of years. Along the way, hostilities developed between families and villages.

Beings from other planets visited the humans of Earth, but did not stay long. Some found the oxygen rich atmosphere of Earth incompatible with their physiology. Others found the lower energies of the planet too dense and worried about contamination of their higher frequency. Others who came during these early times dismissed early humans as too primitive to be of any interest.

Dark energies from the experiments of Atlantis, that had remained on Earth during the long period of dormancy and re-creation of the planet, amplified in the early humans of Earth energies of fear, separation, and domination. This contributed to the physical beings seeing themselves as separate from each other, as opposed to closely linked. They began to judge each other and sought ways to overpower each other. Only those within the immediate family were considered reliably friendly, and then not always.

As humans multiplied in the ensuing years they migrated further and further to many areas of your planet. We created additional physical types to test the best, and worked with the Planetary Oversouls as they infused each new creation with a soul suitable for their primitive lifetimes.

This was the beginning of the experiment to determine how lower conscious humans would evolve into high conscious beings of light. It was conducted under the guidance of Great Beings of Light, conducted with the full cooperation of my Collective of Planetary Creator Gods and the Collective of Planetary Oversouls.

After several hundred thousand years of your time, we

concluded that the species we had created needed additional upgrades, if they were to evolve into higher dimensions of consciousness. To assist us, my Collective invited beings from coherent star systems to contribute their higher energies and DNA.

The beings from these star systems were quite happy to cooperate in all of this, as they had been the beneficiaries of Earth's Christ Consciousness during its Golden Era. The beings from the coherent star systems were of high consciousness because they had maintained it during the period of Earth's dormancy and the billions of years of Earth's resurrection.

With great love and high energies, this was undertaken in several separate locations so that the unique characteristics of each off-world race could be developed. This is the origin of the different races of Earth. Needless to say, human beings at this stage of their development were still quite primitive by your current standards.

At the same time, different physical forms were introduced by the process of allowing off-planet beings to mate with the somewhat evolved original beings. This resulted in several different humanoid forms. These activities also resulted in the stories of gods coming to Earth, and the creation of religions to worship them.

At that time, beings from planets that had been infected by dark energies and who did not adhere to the Schematic of Source, increased their visits to Earth. They sent exploratory expeditions to identify natural resources unique to Earth. They sought to enslave the primitive population of the planet and use them to harvest these resources. Residual memories about gods mating with humans and enslaving them can be traced to imprints of the activities of these infected extraterrestrials.

After many years of experiments, it was decided that a single human form would be most beneficial. Beings from coherent star systems recognized the wisdom of this decision and, thus, the forerunner of current human form was determined. This was done despite the differences in skin color and psychology that had been contributed by beings of the different star systems.

Beings from the dark planets did not agree with the cooperative activities to create a single human form. They vowed not to vanish from Earth, or lose their desire to exploit its resources. Rather, they promoted ways to utilize dark energies to ensnare individual humans. They appeared from time to time in physical form, even though they could not live long in Earth's atmosphere. This process has continued to this time. It has given rise to stories of evil aliens with vastly different physical forms.

✱✱✱✱✱✱✱✱✱✱

I now comment on what we see in your world of today. In certain parts of your world we see populations based in fear and domination.

Politicians and governments are structured to control the physical environment and populace for the benefit of the wealthy and powerful, rather than being at one with the majority of the population and the environment.

Reliance on scientific proof has caused many to avoid opening themselves to the larger picture, to innovative ways of thinking, and to the non-physical.

Modern medicine focuses on keeping people alive, rather than viewing illness as a sign that the soul wishes to retire from this lifetime.

Much farming and raising of animals is about maximizing financial rewards, rather than seeing the opportunities to cultivate the land and interact with animals in a loving experience.

The media is focused on emphasizing fearful aspects of your society, rather than pointing out the positive actions of people who live quiet lives based on love and oneness with all.

Religions focus on the differences between their beliefs, rather than encouraging their followers to accept and love all people as brothers and sisters. Religious dogma and the attitudes of religious leaders seek to create a highly structured belief system based on judgment of others rather than encouraging all to love each other unconditionally.

We see parallels with Atlantis and those who opposed the Schematic of Source favoring their own self-centered visions and buoying their own status. This led to the lowering of consciousness and the self-destruction of the planet then; it can lead to the same again. These demonstrate infection by the residual dark energies of Atlantis.

We also see highly conscious individuals who are focusing their energies to evolve Earth back to her prior stature as a 12th Dimension planet of Light, Love, and Unity. Most of these groups are not as well organized as those opposed to Christ Consciousness, nor do they have coherent paths to achieve their goals.

From our perspective as those who had been involved in Earth's original 12th Dimension creation and the re-creation of this planet and its humans at 3rd Dimension, we are encouraged by recent developments such as the return of Christ Energy to the center of the Earth. For us, this signals the opinion of many nonphysicals that it is very likely that Earth will continue on her path of returning to her former glory days of the Golden Era. It may require many years to fully implement a restoration of Earth to a planet of Christ Consciousness, however, the path is being shown.

We see the inevitable choosing of all to live according to the Schematic of Source, for after all there is no other way. Source is All There Is. The abnormality in this sector of the Milky Way will eventually return to Christ Consciousness.

It makes us sad to see what has become of the beautiful planet and her inhabitants that we created in 12th Dimension so very long ago. We watched helplessly as the planet fell in the Great Catastrophe. We watched during the time of Earth's dormancy. We participated in the re-creation of the planet and with great care created the first of the new humans. We have watched with great pride as those first humans multiplied and struggled upward, albeit sometimes very slowly. Now we watch as some of this generation of humans seek to overcome all and restore Earth to her Golden Era.

These words reflect my experiences with creating the planet and my observations about Earth and her human beings. I am very pleased with the activities of my Collective of Planetary Creator Gods and what we have created. I look forward to celebrating the resurrection of Earth as a 12th Dimension planet of Love and Unity.

I send my blessings to all,
Actin

MK: The information presented by Actin is as grand as the creation of Earth and as specific as the creation of an individual human being. It gave me insights into events in the long history of our planet beginning with its Golden Era. It changed how I see myself and how I see the myriad beings that populate galaxies. We are here on this planet for a brief lifetime, then we are free to migrate anywhere in the universe.

I have encountered many stories about the history of Earth and humanity. Initially they came from my conservative Catholic upbringing. There are theories about Earth from a geological point of view. There are theories based on evolution and chaos. There are beliefs that humans descended from apes. There are stories from indigenous peoples. Most of these stories and theories are based on the narrow vision of 3rd or 4th Dimension, a vision that sees Earth as the only inhabited planet. There are those who listen for faint radio waves coming from the galaxy in hopes of finding that one other planet with intelligent life like Earth.

Actin

Then I found stories about the influence of extraterrestrials and their activities on ancient Earth as they sought to enslave humans to help with gold mining.

Then I experienced many instances of extraterrestrial phenomenon and began to see my planet as one of many inhabited ones.

Over the last 9 years I have come to understand the larger reality from a non-physical point of view. I learned about the involvement of Great Beings of Light in the creation of Earth and the creation of this physical universe. I learned about Earth's Golden Age and about the Fall of Consciousness, a.k.a. The Great Catastrophe.

In this chapter, a Planetary Creator God presents the history of Earth from his perspective. Finally, I have found revelations about Earth that make sense.

✶✶✶✶✶✶✶✶✶✶

Actin's perspective on the initial creation of Earth outside the creation of the Milky Way Galaxy gives new meaning to the contention that Earth is a special planet. This new perspective helped me to better understand why there are people dedicated to restoring Earth to its former glory as the beacon of the Milky Way Galaxy. For it is by moving Earth forward that we can overcome the dark energies that infect people, dragging them away from Christ Consciousness. Going further, I now see that we can impact all the dark planets in this sector of the Galaxy. This gives new meaning to my life, another reason to embrace the higher consciousness of Christ Energy.

Earth's Golden Era was billions of years ago. The original Lemuria and Atlantis were billions of years ago. Earth's re-construction as a 3rd Dimension planet and her evolvement took billions of years after Earth's Great Catastrophe. Humans were introduced to Earth 500,000 years ago. I have trouble comprehending these long times. Yet, we, the humans of today, are the result of them. This is our heritage. This impacts who I am. It makes me appreciate the soul that is driving my physical vehicle and the many incarnations it has had.

The Great Catastrophe was certainly a bump in the road for the Schematic of Source, as applied to this planet and the Milky Way Galaxy. I can only imagine how the loss of the premier planet of the Galaxy reverberated throughout the universe. The carry-over from the Great Catastrophe is still affecting each of us today as we struggle with our everyday lives, not to mention the challenges of finding our way to higher consciousness.

That Earth was re-created to begin the laborious process of ascending back to 12th Dimension certainly explains a lot about why we are here. We volunteered to be here at this time to assist the resurrection of the planet. It may not happen quickly, but then nothing does in universe time. After receiving Actin's communication, I now see how we can influence the outcome of Earth's resurrection by raising our energies.

Dark energies resulting from the mis-directed experiments of Atlantis were present at the re-creation of 3rd Dimension Earth. Like an invading cancer they affect humanity today. It helps to explain why people get trapped in the fear, separation, and domination of the 3rd Dimension. The effects of these energies are all too visible in those committed to power and wealth.

99.9% of the universe does not even know about our 3rd Dimension existence or dark energies. When the rest of the universe is of higher consciousness, it puts any discussion about the dark energies of Earth and the Milky Way Galaxy in a whole new light.

This makes me very grateful for the training I have received, training that has led me to higher consciousness, training that was suggested by my benevolent extraterrestrial friends. Understanding

Actin

that other planets in the Milky Way Galaxy once depended on the Christ Consciousness of Earth to guide them helps me understand why some extraterrestrial races are now willing to help humanity. This puts a different light on extraterrestrials who are here to assist us.

✦✦✦✦✦✦✦✦✦✦

Actin comments that his Collective sees parallels between the current civilization of Earth and that of Atlantis, primarily from the standpoint of ignoring the Schematic of Source and living in fear, separation, and domination. While there are small groups of humans dedicated to living according to Christ Consciousness, the majority of humanity is at 4th Dimension where they may not be trapped in the gut-wrenching fear of 3rd Dimension, but they fail to appreciate the full beauty of living in the Light, Love, and Unity of higher consciousness.

Actin's explanation for the different races on Earth helps me understand that we humans of Earth are all brothers and sisters. We came from a common ancestry. Those distant ancestors were first created by Creator Gods and then modified by the beneficial activities of off-planet beings with an intent to assist our evolution. So much would change, if we saw each other in this way.

Those who rely on their rational minds for all that they believe to be true are missing out on the larger aspects of reality, as represented by non-physical beings. As Actin explains, our planet was created and developed by non-physical beings such as himself. Our souls, that are much greater than our physical bodies, are non-physical. Source and all the myriad beings who created the universe are non-physical. There is no scientific proof for what is written in this book. As long as one demands scientific proof, one is limited to physical reality, and ascension to higher consciousness is impossible.

Actin

I now appreciate how the rest of the universe sees us differently than we see ourselves. Life is so different with the larger picture.

People living in 3rd and 4th Dimensions, who see Earth as the only inhabited planet, and who fail to see the larger picture as communicated by Actin, may mistakenly be referring to a Creator God of this planet when they use the term "God."

Actin's comment about time caused me to understand how it is that we can "feel" changes in energy and time. They are all artificial constructs for our lives in 3rd Dimension, in contrast to the reality of the non-physical that created them.

We are involved in an experiment to evolve the consciousness of human beings. It is unique in that it has not been attempted before with the assistance of so many non-physical beings.

Finally, and certainly of no less importance, there is the realization that I am communicating with a Great Being of Light who formed the beach upon which I walk and the ocean that splashes upon it. He created many of the plants and animals that I care for and enjoy. He makes it possible for me to have nourishing food and water. And long, long ago he created my very distant relatives. Just the fact that I can communicate with someone so wonderful is truly amazing. I am very grateful.

Thank you, Actin, for your communication.

Blessings,
Mark

Questions about Actin's communication:

- What was Earth's Golden Era?

- Why was Earth recreated as a 3rd Dimension planet?

- What was Actin's role for the new Earth?

- How long ago were the first humans created?

- What does Actin's information mean to you?

Adama

Adama

Adama

I am Adama, High Priest of Telos. We are a community of about one hundred thousand who live beneath Mount Shasta, in California, U.S.A.

Some 25,000 years ago our souls approached the Planetary Creator Gods of Earth with a request. They asked that a special place be constructed for them to return to Earth and function as a community. They had been incarnating on other planets of the Milky Way Galaxy since the Great Catastrophe had rendered Earth uninhabitable. They wished to return to Earth to assist with her resurrection back to a 12th Dimension planet of Light, Love, and Unity.

They did this as a group of souls who had occupied the physical forms of beings of Lemuria during Earth's Golden Era, a few billion years previously. A group of souls from ancient Atlantis, of that same period, did the same. In both cases they numbered a hundred individual souls. Both groups wished to have communities separate from the humans of Earth, so that they might live in a higher state of consciousness.

After deliberations lasting many years, the Planetary Creator Gods determined that a site under Mount Shasta, a fourteen-thousand-foot peak in northern California, would be an ideal place to construct such a community. Five other inner-Earth locations were selected in which former Lemurians and Atlantians could develop cultures removed from the human surface dwellers. The Planetary Creator Gods created an idyllic environment and suitable physical forms for the beings who would inhabit each location. The Planetary Oversouls, with whose cooperation these plans had developed, agreed to place souls in the high consciousness adult physical forms when they were completed.

A multitiered city was created under Mount Shasta. Our

ancestors were provided with space in which they would create homes and community arrangements, tiers for growing food if we so wished, a tier for natural recreation, plus abundant water and light. With their high consciousness, our ancestors were able to create whatever necessities of life they desired by simply intending it to happen. In order to avoid interference with the evolutionary process of the surface dwellers, they agreed to remain in these inner-Earth communities, lending their energies to the surface dwellers, until they had ascended to a consciousness that would allow favorable interactions. They named their inner Earth community Telos.

✱✱✱✱✱✱✱✱✱✱

Within the last two hundred years, we have emerged from beneath our inner Earth city on occasion to sample the surface dweller's level of consciousness in person, rather than depending on indirect observations. We are most anxious to openly mingle with surface dwellers when the time is right.

Along with non-physical beings and benevolent extraterrestrials, we stand ready to support the efforts of all surface dwellers who assist the resurrection of Earth. To this end we are available through telepathic communications to interact with individuals to offer our observations and support. We direct positive energies to surface dwellers, particularly those who acknowledge us, in order to support their efforts to raise consciousness. Most importantly, we offer a model of living in high consciousness for all surface dwellers. It has enabled us to consistently deflect dark energies.

Many who occupy Telos today consider the time of Lemuria to date from 25,000 years ago. Physical beings who were created in more recent times have no memory of Earth's Golden Era. Only those of us who are descended from the original inhabitants of Telos have imprints of being incarnated during those ancient times of several billion years ago. Our larger population finds it more to their liking to think in terms of 25,000 years ago as the time of Lemuria.

During these 25,000 years, those of us from Telos and other inner-Earth communities interacted with higher consciousness surface dwellers in Egypt and Tibet to provide them with certain understandings of higher consciousness. These interactions did not continue because they began to view us as gods and sought to worship us.

We now interact with surface dwellers principally through telecommunications, although some humans have glimpsed our star craft materializing, as they emerge from Mount Shasta. We have the ability to travel beyond the confines of Earth and interact with extraterrestrial beings. This is part of the cooperative effort to uplift the surface dwellers of Earth and stall further incursion of dark beings and dark energy.

None of the souls who petitioned the Planetary Creator Gods to create communities for us were involved in the experiments that led to the near destruction of Earth, the Great Catastrophe. The souls who were incarnated during those times and have integrated into our bodies can recall Earth's Golden Era. They watched from quiet times with Oversouls and from distant planets as Earth went dormant, and then later when she was restarted at 3rd Dimension. Our souls maintained contact with each other while they waited the billions of years, until relatively recent times, to establish a community such as Telos.

We very much look forward to the day when we can openly walk the surface of Earth and interact with surface dwellers of higher consciousness. For now, we content ourselves with our very lovely existence in inner Earth.

Light for our community is supplied by giant crystals that

function somewhat like the light emitting diodes surface dwellers use, only much larger. We have a very consistent climate supplied by Earth, as well as pure water from deep aquafers.

We have gardens and orchards where we grow all manner of vegetables and fruits. Despite our ability to materialize what we require, some of us enjoy the experience of growing things. We also have animals which supply us with eggs and milk. We do not consume the flesh of either birds or mammals.

Our families are much like those of surface dwellers. We do mate and produce children. Our children are important to us, as we maintain our high consciousness in the face of energies coming to us from surface dwellers and attempts by dark energies to infect our communities. Most of us live for several hundred years, and usually reincarnate back here. At this time, we have several hundred Planetary Oversouls close by.

Somewhat like us, other planets in the Milky Way Galaxy have their entire civilizations under the surface of the planet. Some of the extraterrestrials who visit us come from such planets and feel right at home among us. They dematerialize their craft in order to land within the confines of Telos.

The temperature of inner Earth is somewhat higher than on the surface, but even the center of the planet is not so high that beings cannot live there. There are very high energy beings living at the center of Earth.

The main difference between surface dwellers and us is that we of Telos function at a high consciousness. Our entire community functions according to Christ Consciousness. We live in unconditional Love and perfect Unity. That is who we are; that is how we live.

Periodically, we have interactions with the other communities of inner Earth, particularly the communities that began life at the same time that we did, 25,000 years ago. There are tunnels connecting the various communities with a total population of all beings of about a million. Although we are in semi-physical bodies, the tunnels make travel more convenient than dematerializing. We have had little interaction with the inner Earth beings who live deeper within the planet and who function at even higher levels of energy.

We were most pleased by the return of the huge Matrix of Christed Energy to the center of Earth. It had been there at the time of the Golden Age, but not since. During Earth's Golden Era, it assisted the planet to model high consciousness for all in the Milky Way Galaxy. At this moment, it is just beginning to bath us in the Golden Light of Love and Unity. That same Golden Light is beginning to be transmitted to all surface dwellers as they slowly gain higher levels of consciousness. We believe that the increasing energy of this Christed Energy Matrix will greatly assist all surface dwellers to higher consciousness. This is a very positive sign for humanity that things are changing for the better. We are most happy to share our higher energy and telepathic communications with high consciousness surface dwellers.

We of Telos are at one with Christ Consciousness. For us that means living in unconditional Love with all, living in perfect Unity with everyone and everything. For example, it means being at one with the land as it grows our fruits and vegetables. We do not dominate the land. This means seeing and working with the land with unconditional Love.

I want to compare this with our observations of most surface dwellers. I offer this not to judge those who live on Earth's surface, but to help them understand what it would be like to live at higher consciousness. We do not wish to lower our energies to meet that of surface dwellers, rather we ask them to raise their energies to meet ours.

The vast majority of those who live on the surface do not regard each other with unconditional Love, even their close family members, let alone loving people of a different race or belief. Few in lower consciousness conceive of benevolent extraterrestrials, let alone inner-Earth beings such as us.

When I say that we function according to Christ Consciousness, this means that we do not have religions where one in authority tells others how to believe. I am a High priest of Telos, but that does not mean that I am a religious figure. Rather, I am one who devotes his entire life to helping others to live according to Christ Consciousness by my example. The vast majority of surface dwellers give away their power to someone whom they believe to be more spiritual than are they and/or they embrace a scientific or spiritual writing that they consider to be inviolate.

We contrast our lives here in Telos with how most surface dwellers live. In them I see much that is fear-based. We see judgment of others and attitudes of better-than or less-than between those who have power and wealth versus those who do not.

✶✶✶✶✶✶✶✶✶✶

Allow me now to compare some details of our lives with those of surface dwellers, for we monitor their actions closely. We see a rise in infections of dark energy, as it struggles to hold onto its control of Earth's population in the face of a general rise in the energy of Love and Unity. As more and more of humanity raise their levels of consciousness, the dark energies franticly exert themselves to combat this. Incidents of terrorism, violence, hatred, and anger are symptoms of the dark exerting itself by infecting the minds of those who are vulnerable. We of Telos are very aware of the dark energies. However, by consistently living with Christ Consciousness, we have deflected it for 25,000 years. Know that living in this way will protect each of you from the energies of fear, separation, judgment, and domination.

Among surface dwellers, dichotomy and judgment is most noticeable in those of positions of wealth and power who fight to retain what they believe is rightfully theirs. Among surface dwellers of the other socio-economic extreme, those in poverty, those fleeing persecution, and those subjected to injustice, are some who live according to Christ Consciousness. Many at lower levels of the socio-economic level live quiet lives of peace and happiness. In recent years, we have seen the majority of humanity edge upward in consciousness, turning away from the allure of power and wealth offered by dark energy in its attempt to retain control.

We contrast our peaceful lives within inner-Earth to the constant struggle experienced by surface dwellers. War and the suffering that accompanies it are the most extreme contrasts with living in Love and Oneness with all. Training soldiers to kill other humans is totally contrary to what Unity means to us. Unity for us means being in complete oneness with everything from the smallest plant to the rocks that surround us to each physical being, and holding them in unconditional Love. We look at surface dwellers in this same way. They are our brothers and sisters despite what they do to each other.

In addition to the killing associated with war, such things as torture, displacement of innocent populations, and the misuse of resources increase the infection ability of dark energy as it feeds from negative thoughts and emotions. Needless to say, a nuclear war would destroy all of the civilization of surface dwellers. It would also affect us in the inner-Earth.

We see much of the media, books, Internet, and educational institutions of surface dwellers directed to supporting the conventional paradigm that ignores Love and Unity. We have no media or Internet as we are in telepathic communications with all in our collective. We have a very different type of education in that it is directed first within the family, then by groups of students who pursue their own agenda.

Most religions of surface dwellers appear to be tightly defined by those who see themselves as somehow more spiritual than ordinary people. Many religions are based on ancient texts that speak with words to the people of that ancient time. We of Telos rely on our ability to directly communicate with non-physical beings who have given us, and continue to give us, concepts and energies of the larger universe and help us to explore who we really are. Surface dwellers could also do this if they would open themselves to wider truths.

The basis of most capitalism as practiced by surface dwellers is the accumulation of wealth and power. Once again, it is contrary to Love and Unity as practiced by those of us in Telos.

Death is the focus of misplaced agonies on the part of surface dwellers. It is the focus of much of their medicine, much of their drama as expressed in books, plays, and movies, and much of the control exercised over the populace by governments and medical systems. The insecurity about death is based on the lack of clarity about life in a physical body, believing that there is nothing beyond the end of one's life.

We of Telos know that reincarnation is fundamental to life in the physical universe. Most of us have memories of past lives, some have memories going back to the time of Earth's Golden Era. This gives us a whole different outlook on death. We see it as a beginning of something new, not an end.

We note that the traditions of many indigenous surface dwellers who have not been integrated into technological and industrial societies are more closely allied to the Love and Unity that is part of Christ Consciousness; this without having been taught about it.

We of Telos support the efforts of all surface dwellers who are seeking higher consciousness, particularly those advocating lives according to Christ Consciousness. We send our positive energy to them, and look forward to interacting with them in person.

We are your brothers and sisters.

Blessings,
Adama

Adama

MK: When I first heard about beings living beneath the surface of our planet, I dismissed it as a fantasy. For me, it was much harder to accept the possibility of people living beneath the surface of my planet than it was to accept the reality of extraterrestrials.

Then I went to a CSETI training in Colorado and, over the course of a week, I saw clear evidence of extraterrestrials. When I saw a craft, bright blue lights blazing, materialize out of the side of Mount Blanca, I became convinced of the reality of beings living beneath the surface of the Earth. At that time, I believed it was an extraterrestrial craft that had materialized as it came out of the mountain. To this day I am still not sure whose craft I saw, extraterrestrial or inner Earth, but I know what I saw and it made a lasting impression.

I have read books referring to Telos and other inner-Earth locations. I had difficulty reconciling what these books and others were saying about its beginning a few thousand years ago, since I was convinced of Lemuria's existence during Earth's Golden Era. Finally, this information from Adama, plus the communication from Actin in the previous chapter, have settled my dilemma.

I appreciate Adama's comparisons between the high consciousness of Telos and the dark energy controlling much of the conventional paradigm in which we live. I agree with all that he said about many surface dwellers living in a civilization focused in fear, separation, and domination. I also see hope for all of my fellow humans as we slowly awaken and climb out of our historic enslavement. I too can see the dark energy escalating its efforts as the quiet voices of many rise to demand new and better ways of thinking and behaving. The comparisons between life in Telos and

Adama

life among us surface dwellers really brought home how far some humans are from functioning according to the Schematic of Source, Christ Consciousness.

Thank you, Adama, for your communication. I hope to visit with you in Telos one day.

Blessings,
Mark

Questions about Adama's communication:

- Do you find the existence of inner Earth beings hard to believe?

- There was an ancient Lemuria during Earth's Golden Era and there are those who date Lemuria from 25,000 years ago. What is the significance of this?

- How does Adama's communication impact your life?

Adrial and Justine

Adrial and Justine

Adrial and Justine

I am **Adrial,** an Overseer of the Andromeda Galaxy. I am one of a collective of Archangels and Overseers established specifically for this Galaxy. I wish to add an Andromedan perspective to what you are receiving from other non-physical Beings of Light. It will assist you to understand this universe from a different point-of-view.

For billions of years we have observed Earth, both during its Golden Era and more recently during its re-creation.

It is okay to see the universe in terms of galaxies, star systems, and planets. However, there are other manifestations of such a grand creation. The Andromeda Galaxy represents such a different way of being.

Visualize existence where there is very little form. Visualize it as fluid or gaseous. See it without edges or dimensions. No depth or context. Yet there is life in this type of form, this way of being, very lively life at much higher frequencies. This is 15th Dimension.

When you see pictures of the Galaxy of Andromeda, you see few clearly defined stars. (Much of this is due to the lack of precision of your telescopes.) Mostly you see what appear to be bright star-like lights. These are the star-planets of Andromeda shining very brightly as if they were stars. However, they are not stars as you have in the Milky Way Galaxy. They are large spherical collectives of individual beings that shine so brightly that they appear to be as bright as a star.

The Galaxy of Andromeda has millions of these brightly radiating star-planets, all of which are inhabited by highly conscious beings. They circle our galactic center somewhat the same as do the stars of the Milky Way Galaxy. However, these star-planets are able to modify their locations within our Galaxy according to the energies put forth by the residents thereof.

Adrial and Justine

The inhabitants of all star-planets of Andromeda are at very high consciousness. All live according to the Schematic of Source, or as you call it, Christ Consciousness.

Mark, you can recall little of your incarnations in Andromeda because our Galaxy exists at 15th Dimension and higher. It is no wonder that you have trouble recalling your incarnations on star-planets of Andromeda because there is nothing to which your rational mind can relate.

Others speak to you about the energies coming from Andromeda rather than from individual planets. This reflects the vaporous condition of much of our Galaxy and a lack of understanding of our star-planets.

The star-planets of Andromeda are the result of the very powerful consciousness of the beings on each, rather than any external phenomenon. The combined energies of the beings are so powerful that they alone create the phenomenon of radiating intense light. They are physical beings but form a tight collective in which they do not appear separate. If you were to view one of these star-planets you would see only the exterior of the collective, the radiating surface. However, below that surface is a collective of millions or billions of individual beings.

It is much like a drop of water in your oceans; the drop disappears within the whole. Yet a drop can emerge by the actions of a wave or evaporation. So it is within the collective of an Andromedan star-planet, beings can emerge when they wish to do so. The physical bodies of Andromedans are very hot. If you were able to come near, they would appear much like a very hot flame of brilliant colors.

Such an arrangement is well within the Schematic of Source for there is perfect Unity within the collective that forms a star-planet, and there is nothing but unconditional Love demonstrated by the beings who make up the collective.

It has not always been this way in Andromeda. At one time we were a galaxy with individual planets. As the energies of individual beings rose so did the temperature of the planet. This continued until planets began to resemble the stars around which they orbited. When the energies of the individual beings on individual planets reached very high frequencies, it was determined to be in the best interests of all to coalesce into the star that the planets were orbiting. This took place throughout the Andromeda Galaxy several billion years ago. These collectives coalesced to the size that would be most advantageous for the beings of the star-planet. Some were larger than others.

The Oversouls of Andromeda are vast Beings of Light for each star-planet has but a few Oversouls due to the high consciousness of the individual flames. The lifetimes of an individual flame can be thousands of years. Each flame determines when it wishes to extinguish. The energies for the collective of flames on a star-planet is provided by tapping the unlimited energy of Source that surrounds all in the universe.

Not all stars of Andromeda had planets, so these remain as individual stars. They are virtually indistinguishable from star-planets.

✦✦✦✦✦✦✦✦✦

Because the collective of a single star-planet is so powerful, its energy is easily shared with lower consciousness beings and collectives such as you have here on Earth. The physical beings of Andromeda are very supportive of the resurrection of your planet. We project our energies to assist you. However, we do not appear as individual beings.

I am speaking to you because your soul has residual energies from your time in a star-planet of Andromeda. Even though your soul is now in a lower energy physical body, you are able to access my Andromedan energy and record my communications.

Adrial and Justine

✱✱✱✱✱✱✱✱✱✱

When Earth was first created, it resembled one of our star-planets in that it shone so brightly that, seen from a distance, it resembled a small star. This bright radiation continued as long as Earth and her inhabitants were in 12th Dimension.

Long ago, during the time of Earth's Golden Era, there were planets in the Milky Way Galaxy where experiments were taking place to determine if dense physicality could be mated with high consciousness. These experiments particularly infected several planets in one sector of the Milky Way Galaxy, causing them to turn away from Source energy.

It was during this time that the planets of Andromeda were just finding their way to higher consciousness. Some beings from the Milky Way Galaxy visited some of these semi-physical planets of Andromeda to determine if experiments could be fruitful there. There were some on a few planets of Andromeda who saw an opportunity to develop something different. They began to experiment with energies that were not aligned with the Schematic of Source.

Because the beings of Andromeda were much different than the physical beings of the Milky Way Galaxy, the experiments were immediately disruptive of the planets on which they were undertaken. This caused several planets to immediately fall into lower energies.

The beings of neighboring planets saw the damage that was occurring. They sent contingents to the errant planets, arguing for a return to Christ Consciousness as displayed by Earth star and their own neighboring planets. After a brief time, the experiments ceased and the errant planets joined a high energy path into consolidation as star-planets.

This occurred long ago, when the planets of Andromeda were

at lower levels of consciousness, were not yet fully consolidated into star-planets, and were vulnerable to adverse external influences. Since that time all star-planets of Andromeda and their physical beings have achieved 15th Dimension or more. There have been no incursions of dark energy.

The star-planets of Andromeda closely resemble Earth during her Golden Era, for at that time Earth and her physical beings radiated sufficient light for the planet to appear as a star. It is because of this that the fall of Earth, and her almost self-destruction, was such a powerful event for all in the universe: The great beacon of Light for the Milky Way Galaxy was extinguished. It is for this reason that the star-planets of Andromeda and their inhabitants feel a closeness to Earth and are intent on assisting her resurrection. We foresee Earth returning to the status of a planet of Light, a star, and will continue to work toward that goal.

✳✳✳✳✳✳✳✳✳✳

Now let me tell you, Mark, a little about the beings, Justine and Moraine, whom you identified as extraterrestrials. You named a planet from which they came based on your investigations. Please understand, when they contacted you, you were coming from a background of writing and speaking about extraterrestrials, so it was natural that you would think of them in that way. You did the same with me, thinking of me as a glorified extraterrestrial and naming me a celestial because you had no other word, and had not yet been introduced to Archangels.

Justine and Moraine were indeed friends who were incarnated in the same star-planet as were you. You had several long lifetimes together. And yes, you did decide to lay down your body and later incarnate in a physical body on Earth. Previously, you had other lives on Earth and you wished to return to it to see how it had changed and to assist its resurrection. You have only a faint memory of this because your level of consciousness cannot deal with more. Justine and Moraine found you on Earth as a result of being onboard an Andromedan star ship in orbit about Earth.

I am most pleased to provide this message for you and will continue to communicate with you in other ways.

Blessings,
Adrial

✶✶✶✶✶✶✶✶✶✶
✶✶✶✶✶✶✶✶✶✶

I am Justine, a being from the star-planet Acer that lies near the center of the Andromeda Galaxy. Although I doubt that you remember it, Acer was once your home, Mark. You and I knew each other during your lifetimes in Acer. By the time you incarnated in Acer it was a star-planet.

I am the one who first contacted you to encourage you to post messages from non-humans on your web site.

As a 15th Dimension being of Light, I have many of the characteristics that you would associate with non-physical beings such as angels. My physicality is so different that you cannot comprehend it from your status as a 5th Dimension being. The physicality of beings in the Andromeda Galaxy, and other galaxies like ours, is so different that it gives new meaning to the term physical.

My star-planet is the home to millions of very high energy beings. The individual light energies of beings on our star-planet are so powerful that Acer radiates with the brightness of a star. If human technology were powerful enough, your astronomers would see Acer through their telescopes and identify it as an individual star. Then they would begin to look for planets around it, but there are no planets. All high energy planets of Andromeda and their beings consolidated into star-planets like Acer, several billion years ago.

We all live very comfortably in Acer and broadcast brilliant light. Acer is not as high a temperature as is your sun. At the same time, we are much warmer than your very dense planet.

It is difficult to describe life on Acer to you so that your lower energy mind will allow you to remember it. This is the reason you have almost no memories of your lifetimes in Acer. I can state this: My life is a perfect expression of the Love of Source. I feel like I am enfolded within a warm blanket and fed nourishing energies as a green plant of Earth would absorb. Despite that comfortable feeling, I have absolute freedom to be whomever and whatever I wish to be. Additionally, I am free to travel anywhere in the universe. This is how you determined that you wished to return to Earth; you visited Earth and observed conditions before making your decision.

I am, at this moment, within your physical space, as you write these words, but you cannot detect my presence. I will not stay long, as it is difficult to be in such low density. Now that a link has been re-established, we may communicate further after I depart from your presence.

I enjoy being with you to observe your life in lower density. I find it most interesting to watch you eat and watch as you write words recording my communication to you. I note your teeth; we have no need for teeth for we have nothing to chew. Neither do we have need of a mouth, for we have nothing physical to consume, nor do we need to speak for all communications are telepathic. We have none of your body functions such as digestion, heart, or lungs for we do not breathe air nor do we have blood. I note your hands. We do not have hands, for we do not touch each other in a physical sense; we feel each other energetically. We do not have a brain, for we function only from our higher mind, a mind linked to Source.

I see that you are asking if we ever have any fun or enjoyment. Obviously, you do not remember. We live in each moment in absolute ecstasy, for we are one with Source and with each other. We are never sad or depressed. We have no need for external pleasures. We have no need for sleep or meditation.

I find the environment in which you live to be most interesting, for we have no such things as dirt or dust. Therefore, we have no need to wash. Nor do we have disease, for there are no dark agents of disease. All in all, I find you and your situation here on Earth very strange, so different than when you were with us in Acer.

I note that you are very committed to assisting the resurrection of Earth to a 12th Dimension planet of Light. I detect others who you know and who are likewise committed. From my perspective it will take the focus of many with such powerful energies to overcome the current infections of darkness in the humans of Earth. I am quite sure that it will happen, perhaps after a period of even greater darkness.

I also observe your personal struggle within the lower energies of Earth; all humans do likewise. After visiting with you, I can understand why you returned to Earth. It does indeed need the assistance of as many light workers as possible to overcome the darkness. At the same time, due to my higher energy I can foresee a time when Earth will finally ascend to higher dimensions. Maybe then it will be time to consolidate your planet into your sun as we of Andromeda have done.

It has been a great pleasure to re-connect with you. I look forward to more conversations.

Blessings,
Justine

MK: What a wonderful surprise these communications

Adrial and Justine

were: First with Adrial, with whom I have had many previous conversations. Next with Justine who says he had known me on Acer. He had previously told me that he had found me after he accompanied an Andromedan star ship into Earth orbit. I well remember his first communication; he convinced me to post my first message.

I was very happy to include Adrial's message in this book. When we had communicated at earlier times, I had understood little of who she really was, so I called her a "celestial" of Andromeda. In the past, she has been most gracious to assist me in a variety of communications. I do not understand how she can appear in these different ways, but I am most grateful for her continuing support. To see the earlier facets of Adrial, visit postings on my web site. I am most grateful for her patience as I slowly evolved to where I now understand who she really is: A Great Being of Light who is an Overseer of the Andromeda Galaxy.

To learn about an entirely new form of a galaxy, made up of star-planets, was initially beyond my imagination. Now that I have had a while to digest it, it makes sense. As we increase in consciousness, our dense physicality will be shed for semi-physical form. Then that semi-physical forms could then transition into other forms as it consolidates into the collective of a star-planet. All the while, the energies that our individual forms emanate would increase to the point that collectively we could consolidate to create a star-like planet, such as 12th Dimension Earth was originally.

I now understand why I have so little recollection of my life in Andromeda. My status as a 5th Dimension being living in a 3rd or 4th Dimension body is simply not compatible with life at 15th Dimension.

I was most pleased to hear from Justine, of whom I have no recollection, except for his communications. This is the case with most all that pertains to my life in Andromeda. As I write these words I am receiving encouragement knowing that the words carry energy. I am hopeful that further conversations with Justine will produce some memories of my lifetime on Acer.

I now understand why others in human bodies have such a difficult time communicating with beings from Andromeda. Some treat them like just another extraterrestrial. Others see them as only energy. It is my understanding that those from Andromeda have utilized extraterrestrials of the Milky Way Galaxy as intermediaries to step down their 15th Dimension energies to be compatible with those of Earth.

I felt strong energies as I typed the words of these communications, and now I read them again. This creates a knowingness within me that I am indeed communicating with my friends from Andromeda.

Thank you Adrial and Justine, for these communications. It was wonderful to re-connect with both of you..

Blessings,
Mark

Questions about
Adrial and Justine's communication:

- Can you visualize a 15th Dimension star-planet?

- How did Earth during her Golden Era resemble a
  star-planet?

- Does Adrial and Justine's communication change your
  concept of the galaxies of the universe?

Es-Su and Alici

Es-Su and Alici

Es-Su and Alici

I am Es-Su, an Archangel of the Pleiades. It is my collective of Archangels to whom physical beings of the Pleiades look for spiritual guidance. We were created by Source specifically for this role in this constellation.

I am here to inform you about our activities as they relate to Earth and to the humans of Earth. During Earth's Golden Era, our constellation had a close association with Earth and the beings who populated Earth Star. When Earth fell from her former glory, it affected all in the Pleiades. Several billion years later, after Earth was re-created in 3rd Dimension, we came to help upgrade her primitive humans.

The stars and planets of the Pleiades constellation were formed during the initial stages of the Milky Way Galaxy by the Galactic Creator Gods. Subsequent to that, Planetary Creator Gods created the initial physical beings after they had molded the planet to become a suitable home for them. Today we are a closely-knit grouping of stars and planets populated by millions of physical beings.

Since the beginnings of our creation, we have remained close to the Schematic of Source, to Christ Consciousness. In the beginning, there were more stars and planets in our constellation. All have coalesced into what is now known in your language as the Pleiades.

The civilization of physical beings of the Pleiades is very old, beginning some nine billion years ago and continuing uninterrupted to the present time. We Archangels have been present since its beginning.

The inhabitants of the Pleiades have never been seriously challenged by the dark energies that invaded nearby planets. Our energies have remained high throughout our existence.

In the earlier days of our creation, the physical beings of the

Es-Su and Alici

Pleiades looked to Earth as a shining example of a planet perfectly aligned with Christ Consciousness, the Schematic of Source. They absorbed Earth's example and created a highly functional civilization on all planets of our constellation.

The initial creation of physical beings in the Pleiades took place on the planet Zeane. There, Planetary Creator Gods created individual physical forms. Planetary Oversouls expressed souls for these beings. In the beginning, only a few were created in this way. They were of a high function. They understood who they were and wished nothing more than to construct a race of conscious physical beings. Thus began the successful propagation of this planet toward what is now millions of beings at high consciousness.

Physical beings were created on Zeane by the Planetary Gods and Planetary Oversouls. They were not imported from another planet, nor were they result of evolution from lower level animals of the planet. They were of high consciousness, but less than the 12th Dimension of Earth. They possessed a much less dense physical form than that of the current humans of Earth.

Life on Zeane was focused around seeing all beings and the environment in Unity. Everything was provided for them. Their 7th Dimension physical bodies were created to hold high consciousness. All was very peaceful. They were shown how to grow and harvest crops. The climate was quite accommodating so there was little need for housing. Seldom did they require repairs to their bodies. All in all, it was a very idyllic situation. It remained so as the population grew and matured.

After a million years, it became obvious that space was needed to expand the growing population of Zeane. This resulted in the development of technology for traveling to the other planets of our constellation. We Archangels assisted this effort by pointing out the design for space craft based on what had been successful on planets of other star systems in the Milky Way Galaxy. The beings of Zeane were then assisted by those who had mastered the technology.

Es-Su and Alici

A program to populate other planets within our constellation began. We had no intention of expanding our population beyond our constellation then and have not varied from that in the billions of years since.

Settlements on the planets of the Pleiades were all completed during Earth's Golden Era. Many beings of these planets visited Earth to absorb the higher energies of her inhabitants and her model of Christ Consciousness. This helped all in the Pleiades maintain their high consciousness in the subsequent billions of years.

The settlement of the planets of Pleiades took place before any planets within the Milky Way Galaxy had been overwhelmed by dark energy. Pleiadians had explored star systems that later came under its influence. Rather than clash with dark energy on these planets, they withdrew.

In subsequent times, we of the Pleiades have erected defenses against intrusion by the dark energy or by beings of planets on which the dark energy is in control. This has been done by constantly maintaining our status as planets of Love and Unity, as a coherent constellation aligned with Christ Consciousness.

During the final moments, as Earth was falling in consciousness, we provided a safe place to store some of the treasures of Lemuria and Atlantis. All in the Pleiades observed with great sadness the fall of Earth.

✶✶✶✶✶✶✶✶✶✶

After Earth was restarted as a 3rd Dimension planet, Pleiadians awaited opportunities to be of assistance. These presented themselves when we were invited to come to Earth to upgrade her human population. Our involvement with the humans of Earth has continued to this time.

We are most interested in the return of Earth to its status as a 12th Dimension Christed planet. We foresee that this will positively impact all planets and beings in the Milky Way Galaxy, particularly those that have fallen into darkness. This will then lift the entire Galaxy to higher consciousness.

I believe this information will assist the humans of Earth to adjust their opinions about beings from other star systems who are your space brothers and sisters. I am happy to have provided it.

Blessings,
Es-Su

I am Alici from the planet Zeane, the originally inhabited planet of the Pleiades, and am what you would term an extraterrestrial. I come to you to explain our role relative to Earth and humanity. We are most interested in assisting the resurrection of your planet, for its struggling situation affects all of us.

There are seventeen inhabited planets associated with the stars of what you call the Pleiades. At this time all of these are coherent in that their inhabitants are aligned with the Schematic of Source.

It was not always like this. We were created so that the inhabitants of the planets would initially function at a somewhat lower dimension. With the assistance of Archangels and Avatars, and the energies coming from Earth, we were able to raise ourselves to a higher dimension. This is where we now reside.

✳✳✳✳✳✳✳✳✳✳

Over the past 200,000 years, we have interacted with the humans of Earth. Initially, we stood by as your primitive ancestors struggled to survive. This condition continued for several hundred thousand years.

At the invitation of the Archangels and the Planetary Creator

Es-Su and Alici

Gods of Earth, we sent a group of our most respected beings to Earth. We wished to explore the feasibility of assisting the upgrade of the humans of Earth by establishing a colony.

We finally determined that we could be of more assistance without a colony. For the next 100,000 years, we worked to transform the brains of the primitive beings using applied energies. We also used biological technology to upgrade their physical bodies. These efforts resulted in upgraded Earth humans that resembled the physicality of our ancestors when they had physical form in somewhat lower dimensions.

Other beneficial extraterrestrial races were also on Earth at that time. They too were involved with upgrading humanity. In addition, there were self-centered extraterrestrials who wished to enslave humans for their own agenda.

To avoid conflicts, each off-planet race carried out its activities in different areas of the planet. Each extraterrestrial race achieved somewhat different results. Those with whom we closely interacted came to resemble our light hair and complexions and blue eyes.

It was proposed that a common form of humans be developed. As we were striving for this, we interacted with dark energy extraterrestrials who were of the 3rd Dimension. They manifested the energies of fear, anger, and domination in their desire to control all on the planet. It was a struggle to interact with them, but for the good of the planets we did so. We wanted the human form to more closely resemble what we were familiar with. They wanted the human form to mimic what they represented.

We started our discussions with concepts very far apart. It required many, many meetings to achieve what you now known as human beings. The biggest stumbling block was the beneficial extraterrestrial's insistence that the human form had to allow for eventual ascent to 12th Dimension. The 3rd Dimension extraterrestrials left the discussions without resolving this issue. The beneficial extraterrestrials went on to reach an agreement on human form. Over the next 50,000 years it evolved into the standard.

Es-Su and Alici

As the lower dimension beings from the dark planets abandoned the discussions, they threatened to continue to get their way. Today, those of dark energies exploit the differences in the races of humanity in an attempt to achieve their goals of planetary domination.

The majority of planetary races in this Galaxy, such as the Pleiadians, support the advancement of humanity. However, you have a few extraterrestrial races interacting with humanity who wish humanity to remain in 3rd Dimension.

In addition to this factor, humanity has dark energy seeking to infect it. This energy had its origins on planets of the Milky Way Galaxy, when physical beings and Creator Gods experimented with integrating high consciousness and physical form outside the Schematic of Source. Lower consciousness races were the result of this. It is the same energy from the days of Atlantis. It remained on Earth through her time of dormancy. It is the dark energy that you see in those who crave wealth and power, who do not see other humans as their brothers and sisters, and do not see all in oneness.

There are several races on your planet. Few are purely of one type body or one mental or psychological type. They are the result of thousands of years of interacting with each other and the influence of extraterrestrials, as I have described.

With the evolution of humanity over the past 200,000 years, the races of Earth today are more similar than they are different. Their human bodies closely resemble each other. There are more differences in cultures than there are in body types.

We of the Pleiades have been involved with several activities during the past 200,000 years. At the instigation of Andromedans, we undertook the construction of pyramids around the planet. These were used as focal points to broadcast energies to specific areas. We constructed these pyramids from rock that was available nearby and fashioned it with our advanced technology, as well as lifting the heavy pieces into place.

In more recent times, we have caused our space craft to become visible in an effort to awaken humans to our presence. We have interacted with specific humans to allow photographing of our ships. We have used holographic projections to create images of our ships. There are no photographs of individual Pleiadians, for that is not possible, as we of the Pleiades are semi-physical.

We of the Pleiades are directly involved with creating crop circles that appear in England and elsewhere.

✶✶✶✶✶✶✶✶✶✶

A fleet of our star ships are currently in orbit about Earth. We are beaming beneficial energies to all on the planet and blocking further intrusions by dark energies.

We will continue to support the ascension of humanity as the only way to restore Earth to its former glory as a 12th Dimension planet, as Earth star.

I am happy to provide this information and hope it will help to raise the consciousness of all.

Blessings,
Alici

MK: I was very happy to have these communications from Es-Su and Alici. I have few comments other than they helped reinforce that there are extraterrestrials of higher consciousness. And they filled a gap in my understanding of the millions of planets in the Milky Way Galaxy.

I am aware of individuals such as Billy Meiers who had extensive contact with the Pleiadians. They directed him to photograph their ships in the 1970s (before digital photography).

Es-Su and Alici

Billy's photos are some of the clearest pictures we have of extraterrestrial craft. The photos were undertaken by special arrangement with the Pleiadians, as many other photos of non-human craft are blurred due to the higher frequencies at which they operate.

I was very happy to receive the material about pyramids and crop circles. There are many theories as to how they have been created. This serves to dispel some of these.

Thank you, Es-Su and Alici, for this communication.

Blessings,
Mark

Questions about
Es-Su and Alici's communication:

- Why is it important that the Pleiadians have maintained their high consciousness over billions of years?

- How have their interactions with humans influenced our lives?

- Does Es-Su and Alici's information change your feelings about extraterrestrials?

An-Ra-Ta

An-Ra-Ta

An-Ra-Ta

I am An-Ra-Ta, of the Collective of Archangels of the Constellation of Sirius. My collective has been integral with the planets and physical beings of Sirius since their initiation several billion years ago.

My Collective watched as the stars and later the planets of the Sirius Constellation were created by the Galactic Creator Gods. We watched as each star was lovingly formed and then observed each planet as it resulted from the spinning of a star. Then physical beings were created by the Planetary Creator Gods, along with the incarnation of souls by the Planetary Oversouls.

Overseeing Sirius was an assignment we were given by Source. We are most pleased with the status of Sirius as a coherent Constellation fully aligned with the Schematic of Source and Christ Consciousness. As a coherent Constellation, we Archangels and all beings of Sirius function in oneness.

Archangels are attached to stars and planets to assist the evolution of the beings therein. We do this in close cooperation with the Planetary Creator Gods and Oversouls, and at times in cooperation with Unique Oversouls, like Aon, who supply special souls to Avatars who set an example of living according to Christ Consciousness.

My primary role as an Archangel of the Sirius Constellation has been to assist the physical beings of the planets of Sirius to maintain their focus on Christ Consciousness. Currently, all beings of the Sirius constellation are of high frequencies. Over the billions of years, since the very beginning of our Constellation, the physical beings of Sirius have maintained their focus on the Schematic of Source. Aligned in higher energies, never have we faltered.

At the present time, there are two stars and seven planets that comprise the Constellation of Sirius. In earlier times there were three stars; one of these was consolidated into Sirius A.

✷✷✷✷✷✷✷✷✷✷

The beings of the Sirius Constellation have had a long history with Earth and her beings. After our star systems and planets were created, and after physical beings were placed thereon, we looked to Earth as an example of the Schematic of Source and Christ Consciousness. Although our physical beings were created at a relatively high level of consciousness, we were not of Earth's 12th Dimension. So, we looked to Earth as a living example and sent individual beings to visit her. Earth, at that time, was a stationary star-like planet of great brilliance. Her 12th Dimension energy was a guide post for all planets of the Milky Way Galaxy.

These peaceful relations continued for several billion years. Our alliance with the beings of Earth was solidified during this time.

✷✷✷✷✷✷✷✷✷✷

Some planets of nearby stars were affected by experiments that explored ways of combining physical form and consciousness that was different than planned by the Schematic of Source. This resulted in the development of dark energies that infected planets beyond those directly involved in the experiments.

When such experiments on Earth created problems, we sent some of our higher energy beings to Earth to convince those who were conducting the experiments to cease. This was of no avail; the experiments continued.

Later we observed beings from Atlantis as they stored certain critical energies deep in the crystals of Earth. This was an attempt to preserve some of the best of Atlantian civilization. We also received some of Earth's most precious examples of Christ Energy.

We remained close to Earth as she stumbled and was almost destroyed by the experiments of those who did not recognize their connection to Source.

We could only watch from afar as Earth almost slipped into total annihilation. Later we observed the time of dormancy, as all life was frozen.

Then we saw her re-created as a 3rd Dimension planet. We watched as Earth was shuttled into its current orbit about your star. We were pleased to see that Earth was placed in a position not too distant from us, versus somewhere on the other side of the Milky Way Galaxy.

All physical beings of Sirius waited patiently for an opportunity to interact and assist, as we saw the creation of the first 3rd Dimension humans. My Collective of Archangels advised patience, as our higher vibrations were not compatible with the primitive beings of Earth.

✦✦✦✦✦✦✦✦✦✦

300,000 years after the first 3rd Dimension humans were created on Earth, my Collective of Archangels was consulted by the Great Overseers of the universe. Would the beings of Sirius be willing to assist primitive Earth humans with our energy? Would we be willing to supply our DNA and mate with the primitives?

Most eagerly, we agreed to undertake this. A small contingent of Sirius's physical beings was dispatched to Earth. It was later followed by a large contingency who remained on Earth in its compatible atmosphere for many years.

An-Ra-Ta

As a representative of my Collective, I went to Earth to help coordinate the activities of the beings from Sirius. I was very actively involved with Earth's Planetary Creator Gods and Planetary Oversouls as they created new human forms based on interactions with the beings of Sirius and infused new souls.

We undertook our work quite apart from other off-planet beings who were here to assist fledgling humanity. The results of our interactions – based on DNA and mating with the primitive beings of Earth – were a race of humans with great strength and durability, somewhat resembling the beings of our Constellation.

While we were unable to advance the brains of humans to where we could plant concepts of the larger picture of the universe and Source, we were successful in conveying the beginnings of the ideas of love, peace, and oneness.

After 50,000 years of interacting with the new humans of Earth, we had developed what we thought would be the physical forms of humans. Along with benevolent beings from other star systems, we searched for a standard human form all could agree upon. We did not agree to incorporate the suggestions of beings from dark planets, even though they had contributed to upgrading the brains of humans. After much discussion and further experiments, a standard human form was agreed upon. Thereafter, all evolution of humanity was based on it.

✶✶✶✶✶✶✶✶✶✶

Over the period of ten thousand to fifteen thousand years ago, the physical beings of Sirius transported the great beings that you call whales and dolphins to Earth. They were physically transported aboard star ships constructed for this purpose. Prior to our actions these beings were not present in your oceans. These wondrous beings remain in contact with their brothers and sisters from Sirius.

An-Ra-Ta

Out of love for humanity, each of these great beings volunteered to come to Earth knowing that in future years they or their progeny might be tortured and/or killed by the humans of Earth. A Planetary Oversoul accompanied this group of beings, who are conscious of who they are and why they came to Earth.

Today, whales and dolphins provide an added ingredient to the energies of your planet. They hold the Light of Source for Earth. They anchor the efforts of off-planet beings who are gathered to assist Earth and humanity at this time. Additionally, they set an example of living at higher consciousness as they demonstrate love and family life. It is most unfortunate that they have been hunted and otherwise misused, yet these loving beings continue to serve humanity.

I trust that my words have contributed to your understanding of the wondrous universe in which you live and the unique planet upon which you reside.

Blessings,
An-Ra-Ta

MK: These words from An-Ra-Ta were most welcome, for they explained yet another part of who we are and from whence we came. And, once again, they emphasize the role each of us can play in assisting the resurrection of Earth.

His revelation about whales and dolphins was a real eye opener. I had incorrectly assumed they were the result of the evolution of species native to Earth. That they had been transported to Earth so recently is quite startling. I had some glimpse of this previously, but An-Ra-Ta's words confirmed once again the ongoing involvement of our star brothers and sisters.

Blessings,
Mark

Questions about
An-Ra-Ta's communication:

- Why are Archangels linked to a constellation such as Sirius?

- How have Sirians interacted with humanity?

- What new species did Sirians supply to Earth?

- How does An-Ra-Ta's information impact your life?

Ea-Ta

Ea-Ta

Ea-Ta

Iam Ea-Ta, an Oversoul of the Collective of Planetary Oversouls of Earth. My Collective was created by Source to provide a soul for the physical body of each human of Earth. We express new souls as well as facilitating souls who are reincarnating with experiences of past lifetimes. We also facilitate the placement of a soul when it incarnates into an existing body as a walk-in. We provide a place where souls who have completed their incarnations may relax and determine their next incarnation.

As you might imagine the activities of my Collective are extensive. There are many, many Oversouls involved, because there are many humans beginning lifetimes on Earth each day. There are also a large number of walk-ins.

My Collective provides the all-important link between the soul and the physical body during incarnations. Souls are not free to occupy human bodies without our involvement. We remain closely allied with each soul throughout its incarnation.

The souls that my Collective expresses or facilitates are always of high consciousness. They are pure non-physical beings of Light who volunteer to associate with a particular physical body for a given lifetime. After its initial expression, each soul lives forever. Many of the souls that we facilitate have experienced many, many lifetimes.

Each soul enters a body to experience certain objectives for a particular lifetime. The term "incarnation" is a bit of a misnomer. If you could measure the size of such a non-physical being, the soul would be much, much larger than the body. A soul does not compress itself to fit within a physical body.

There is no specific number of souls with whom a Planetary Oversoul may interact. The number is dependent on a number of factors such as levels of involvement with the number of souls in its care and the environments in which the physical bodies reside.

Ea-Ta

A soul having a challenging life requires more attention than one experiencing a peaceful lifetime. The same is true for a soul in a difficult environment.

✳✳✳✳✳✳✳✳✳✳

After Earth's initial 12th Dimension physical beings were firmly established, my Collective became responsible for providing souls to subsequent generations of these highly conscious physical beings. Because there were no souls that had retired from previous lifetimes on Earth and there were no other planets from which such high consciousness souls could migrate, new souls were manifested. The original 12th Dimension physical beings of Earth are sometimes referred to as Adam Kadman.

It was during this time, Mark, that your soul was first created. My Collective of Planetary Oversouls retained a relationship with your soul, as it reincarnated on Earth. When it incarnated on other planets, a Planetary Oversoul there assumed that relationship. Such relationships occur with all souls that are incarnated in physical beings.

✳✳✳✳✳✳✳✳✳✳

At the initiation of Earth eons ago, souls that incarnated in physical bodies were all attuned to living in 12th Dimension bodies. It was our task to assist newly expressed souls to find a desirable physical form among those being created by the Creator Gods. In subsequent times, we focused on finding a suitable physical form in which to carry out the next experiences souls desired. For the next billion years, this was not particularly challenging because both the planet and the physical beings were of 12th Dimension consciousness.

This situation was different from the other planets of the Milky Way Galaxy. On these other planets there were ample opportunities to select among a variety of lives with different experiences.

Ea-Ta

From the very beginning, my Collective was well aware that the goal of Earth and her residents was to be a living model of the energies of the Schematic of Source for other planets in the Milky Way Galaxy. With that goal in mind, we sought to construct ideal life situations for the souls of the physical beings of Earth.

This was done in cooperation with the specially chosen Collective of Planetary Creator Gods who were supplying the physical forms into which we would incarnate souls. With both high energy souls and high energy physical bodies, it was quite easy to integrate a soul with an intended body. There was virtually little distinction between the two, because high consciousness souls easily integrate into highly conscious physical forms. This resulted in extraordinarily beautiful beings in every way, ideal representations of Christ Consciousness.

Highly conscious physical beings living on highly conscious planet Earth existed for a billion years. I recall many, many long periods of tranquility during this time. This was known as Earth's Golden Era. It was during this time that the civilizations of Lemuria and Atlantis were present on Earth.

It was also a time that groups of souls were forming so that subsequent incarnations of members of a soul group could take place in a family or other group of physical beings. This continued for many incarnations. It is common in your time also, with souls choosing different roles within a family, within a group of friends, and/or different roles within a society. Sometimes a soul will enter the body of a male, the next time that of a female; one time a parent, the next time a child; a leader, then a follower; an abuser, then a victim.

Unlike the Creator Gods who can start a lineage and allow it to grow, thereby producing new physical humans, we Oversouls must be directly involved in providing the soul for each new human. We do not create a lineage of souls replicating themselves, although there are many souls wishing to reincarnate. Nevertheless, each incarnation is an individual decision.

Ea-Ta

✳✳✳✳✳✳✳✳✳✳

I now move forward to the time when certain Creator Gods and some of the physical beings of Earth were experimenting with integrating high energies and dense physical forms, as previously described by Actin. When it became evident that Earth would continue its downward spiral, the Christ Consciousness was removed from the center of the planet. Thus, there was no high consciousness model for the beings of the planet.

There were a variety of physical beings, from those of lower energies, who were involved with the experiments, to those who of higher energy, who were not involved. These remained on Earth in hopes of a love-based outcome.

There were many opinions about the experiments. Some believed that the experiments were worthwhile; others objected to them as clear violations of the Schematic of Source.

From the perspective of my Collective, it was most difficult to find suitable physical beings to accommodate high energy souls in the midst of the experiments. Some souls wanted nothing to do with incarnating into physical beings in families who were committed to the experiments. Others wanted to walk-in to the families of the perpetrators of the experiments to convince them to go a different way.

Facilitating souls for newborn children of parents opposed to the experiments presented a different challenge, for their projected lifetimes were much in question. This was particularly true in Lemuria where the experiments of the Atlantians were causing their side of the planet to fall to lower frequencies than they had ever experienced. We Oversouls could see that the future of Lemuria was tenuous and the future of the children could not be predicted. We counseled against incarnations in children of Lemuria at this time. Nonetheless, there were souls who insisted on incarnating for the experience.

In the final days of Lemuria, many souls fled their physical bodies. We provided welcome relief for those who had been accustomed to lifetimes in high energy physical bodies, but saw their bodies facing unexpected difficulties as the planet shifted beneath them.

During the final moments of what was to be the near self-destruction of the planet, brought on by the continuing experiments in Atlantis, we counseled souls to refrain from incarnating there. Thus, the birth rate dropped dramatically due to the lack of willing souls.

The final demise of Atlantis took some time as the experiments continued and Earth reacted to them. This became a fast-paced time for my Collective as many souls left their bodies either intentionally or as the result of death due to the experiments. All souls, whether their physical bodies had taken part in the experiments or opposed them, were welcomed and given opportunities for recuperation after their strenuous lifetimes.

✶✶✶✶✶✶✶✶✶✶

After the Great Catastrophe, there were no incarnations on Earth for the planet was in a state of suspended animation. This was a time when many souls who had returned to Oversouls sought out incarnations on other planets, while they awaited the decision of the Overseers and Creator Gods as to the disposition of Earth. Many of these souls wished to incarnate with souls that had been with them in Lemuria or Atlantis. We tried to accommodate this whenever possible.

When it was finally decided that Earth would be restarted at a 3rd Dimension level, the souls of the former planet were faced with decisions of how to occupy themselves for a few billion years as the planet was evolved and prepared to accommodate new physical beings. This assumed that they had any interest in returning to a new Earth.

Many long discussions revolved around opportunities to incarnate on other planets, how long to plan on such a path, what were the options in terms of other planets, where were they located, what would a new Earth look like, and did they want to return to incarnate on a planet of low energy.

Those who were committed to Christ Consciousness sought out planets that had benefitted from Earth's example. There were now many coherent planets in the Milky Way Galaxy. Although I advised against it, those souls who wanted to continue with the experiments sought out incarnation opportunities on planets within this sector of the Galaxy where the experiments were continuing.

Understanding that each Oversouls could not encompass the myriad demands of all of the souls to which we were connected, each member of my Collective determined which planet it wished to be associated with and went about collecting souls of that orientation. This was most unusual because some souls, who had been with a specific Oversoul for many millions of years, over many incarnations on Earth, were now to associate with a new Oversoul.

We were split in several directions depending on the souls we had collected. My orientation was to find a high energy planet that I could suggest to my experienced souls. Thus, I entered into several billion years of offering the former souls of Earth incarnations in Sirius, the Pleiades, and other coherent planets throughout the Milky Way Galaxy.

✶✶✶✶✶✶✶✶✶✶

When the new Earth was ready for the introduction of human forms, I volunteered to be one of the Planetary Oversouls in a newly established Collective that would facilitate souls for the new humans. This was a different challenge, as souls would be associated with immature physical forms.

None of the souls who had been present on Earth during her

Golden Era volunteered to undertake this experience. It was not surprising as these souls had experienced many lifetimes over the five billion-year interim in the higher consciousness physical beings of higher consciousness planets. Also, they were most concerned that their souls, which had experienced living at high energy, would somehow be damaged by being incarnated in low energy physical beings.

So, my Collective began to express new souls specifically to enter into lower energy physical bodies. Even then, it was a challenge to match a newly manifested soul that had a high energy with a 3rd Dimension body. This was accomplished by having the soul reside outside the physical body, rather than be integrated within, as was the case in higher consciousness physical bodies.

After some 400,000 years had passed on the new Earth, the consciousness of humanity had risen so that some of my flock, who had been on Earth at the time of Atlantis and Lemuria, wished to once again incarnate in the physical bodies of the beings of Earth. They saw this as an experiment and recognized that the environment on Earth, as well as the physical bodies, would be quite different from what they had been used to on planets of higher consciousness. Nonetheless, some plunged into the experiment with great enthusiasm, intending to upgrade the consciousness of all with whom they interacted, thereby assisting the resurrection of Earth.

✶✶✶✶✶✶✶✶✶✶

Turning now to present-day Earth, for each new physical body being born there are usually several souls who wish to incarnate on Earth. Sometimes they are souls who have had prior lives on Earth and wish to revisit to complete experiences, or wish to have the opposite experience to gain from that perspective. Other times, they may have been incarnating on other planets and are seeking the uniqueness of an experience on Earth. We express a new soul for an incarnation when there is no match between existing souls and a particular physical body.

An incarnation is a coordinated choice between the soul wishing to incarnate with its desires for new experiences and the Oversoul who provides opportunities based on its knowledge of the physical bodies available. First comes defining what a soul wishes from an incarnation, then comes seeking appropriate physical bodies. Despite our ability to see the future of a given body, this is always a guess because there are so many factors that enter into the life of an Earth human: free will, accidents, unanticipated events, and perseverance. Seldom does a lifetime play out exactly as foreseen when a soul is determining if it wants to incarnate in a particular body.

Then there is the selection of a soul from the several who wish an incarnation in a particular body. Here it is the task of the Oversoul to decide, based on the highest good for all involved.

In years past, say a thousand years ago, when there were fewer people on Earth, our task as Oversouls was somewhat easier. First, there were fewer choices for a soul in terms of the number of physical beings. Second, there was less demand due to a smaller number of souls seeking to incarnate. During the last two hundred years, the population of Earth has exploded due to new technologies and extended lifetimes. Third, now it is recognized that Earth is entering its final stage of transformation and many souls wish to be a part of this.

Many millions of Planetary Oversouls are active on Earth at the current time. We are somewhat specialized into Collectives according to the characteristics of the physical bodies and their expected lifetimes. Oversouls who supply souls with longer expected lifetimes have quite a different approach than Oversouls who supply souls for physical bodies with lifetimes of a few months or years.

Other considerations involve the levels of love versus fear in perspective physical bodies. We carefully consider the general consciousness of a projected lifetime and the opportunity a soul might have to upgrade the consciousness of the physical body. In other words, we specialize so as to maximize our service to the souls with whom we are involved, both those we are seeking to find a suitable physical body, as well as those we have already placed into a physical form.

While it is likely that, over the course of a soul's many incarnations, it may associate with many Oversouls, at the same time some souls are facilitated by the same Oversoul over and over.

The task of providing souls for children of today is much different than it was a thousand years ago. There are many more considerations today as to what a soul might encounter during a lifetime.

Let me use religion as one example. Years ago, there were few religious choices for an individual. Most people followed the religious lead of their parents: Catholic, Buddhism, Hinduism, Jewish, or Islam. Today there are many religious choices, particularly in a country like the United States. Here there are a number of different denominations of Christian churches. In addition to a selection of churches, an individual in the U.S. has an opportunity to belong to any number of spiritual organizations. At the opposite extreme, some countries seek to control the religion of their populations, thereby limiting choices for a perspective soul.

If it is foreseen that a particular human form is not expected to live in the country or family in which it was born, then the decision of the soul becomes increasingly complex.

A somewhat similar situation arises when a soul is seeking an experience within a wealthy family as opposed to a poor one, or a rural lifestyle versus a city, or the life of an educated person versus a lifetime without schooling. Then there are the issues of forecasted health. What is likely to happen with sickness or injuries? The issue of a difficult lifetime, where a soul is seeking difficult experiences, is most challenging because it involves making projections about lifestyles, illnesses, and death. Last, but not least, is the desire of souls to incarnate in families or situations that will lead to lifetimes with souls with whom they have previously incarnated.

My task as an Oversoul, along with that of all Oversouls who are assisting souls to find suitable human forms, is to be as helpful as possible without unduly influencing the choices made.

The souls of some Earth humans have had many lifetimes, beginning when Earth was first populated billions of years ago. Imagine for a moment, the number of lifetimes there could be in a billion years, in ten billion years. Then picture the number of different experiences that a soul accumulates during these many lifetimes. Viewing your current lifetime from this perspective certainly changes how you see yourself, how you choose to live.

Since the early years of Earth's Golden Era, many souls have repeated incarnations on Earth. Many of you who are reading these words have souls that incarnated originally in Earth's Golden Age, then went on to incarnate on other high consciousness planets, then incarnated sometime in Earth's history as a 3rd Dimension planet, and are now incarnating on Earth once again. Some of you, like Mark, have incarnated on Earth multiple times, interlacing these Earthly incarnations with lifetimes on other planets

At this moment, as has been the case for many years, each soul that incarnates on Earth has a mission to uplift the planet and its humans to higher consciousness. This is true for each and every soul incarnating on Earth. It is fixed at the moment of the incarnation. It can be an incarnation into the birth of a new physical being, or it can be a walk-in to a mature physical body. In each case there is an understanding that the primary mission for this lifetime is to uplift humanity. The soul incarnates with this understanding and influences the physical body to live it regardless of the subsequent circumstances of the physical being's incarnation. During its incarnation, the soul broadcasts higher consciousness unconsciously to all physical beings with whom the individual comes into contact.

Ea-Ta

Mark, when your soul was handed-off from an Oversoul in Andromeda, at your request to return to Earth, I was the Oversoul who received it. At your soul's request, your soul and I immediately began to examine opportunities for a soul exchange. I presented three such opportunities where a soul, for various reasons, was willing to vacate a body so that a new soul could enter. At that moment, there were only a few such opportunities.

One of these involved a life-threatening accident with only a little hope of full recovery of the physical body. The second was the body of a woman who had recovered from cancer but was far from healthy. The third was the one your soul chose.

We examined the family situation as well as the foreseen health of your body. We foresaw many of the events that have occurred since the soul exchange. We also saw an opportunity to upgrade the consciousness of your physical lineage compared to what it had been experiencing.

Of principal concern was the placement of a soul that had experienced lifetimes in the 15th Dimension of Andromeda into a body deeply immersed in 3rd Dimension. The risk of contamination was pointed out; nevertheless, you decided to proceed. Many of the difficulties you experienced during your subsequent years were largely a reflection of this compatibility issue.

I have remained close over the intervening years, offering insights on occasion – a quiet voice that you sometimes heeded.

We trust you have learned from this discourse that souls volunteer to incarnate in the bodies of their choice, and incarnate whenever and wherever they see an opportunity to gain specific experiences during a lifetime. Souls are very specific in these requests. We Planetary Oversouls accommodate their wishes to the greatest extent possible, even handing them off to other Planetary Oversouls when they wish to incarnate in a different Earth situation or on a different planet. Keep in mind that we are dealing with time in billions of years and incarnations of any one soul numbering in the hundreds or thousands.

It has been my pleasure to have communicated with you, Mark. I look forward to continuing our relationship.

Blessings,
Ea-Ta

✶✶✶✶✶✶✶✶✶✶
✶✶✶✶✶✶✶✶✶✶

MK: I first learned about oversouls after my awakening in 1988. In the years since, I have encountered several different ways in which people define oversouls. At best, the definition of an oversoul seems to be fuzzy and the subject is overlooked in many spiritual teachings.

Merriam Webster Dictionary defines oversoul as: the absolute reality and basis of all existences conceived as a spiritual being in which the ideal nature imperfectly manifested in human beings is perfectly realized.

The American Heritage College Dictionary defines oversoul as: In New England transcendentalism, a spiritual essence or focus in the universe in which all souls participate and that transcends individual consciousness.

References to oversouls are found in books about near death experiences, soul mates, soul groups, reincarnation, and in some spiritual communities. They are always with few specifics; nothing approaching this information from Ea-Ta.

I encountered the word "oversoul" during my last nine years of training to achieve higher consciousness. Some of what has been communicated by Ea-Ta was somewhat familiar, but there was nothing in my training from the perspective of an Oversoul. This is new ground for me. My view of Oversouls has been redefined by the communications from Ea-Ta.

I now define an Oversoul as a Great Non-physical Being that expresses (creates) souls, cares for individual souls that are incarnated in physical beings, and facilitates the placement of souls into bodies chosen by the souls after extensive investigations. By virtue of their awareness of numbers of souls and physical bodies, existing and being born, Planetary Oversouls keep abreast of incarnation opportunities. Oversouls also implement the situation of a walk-in. They contact a soul that wishes to walk out, and facilitate the exchange.

My understanding is that Source provides a unique directive for each soul. Oversouls are informed of this and remind an individual soul of this mission when it is seeking a new incarnation and during its current lifetime.

In summary, Oversouls are charged with keeping track of physical bodies that are available for incarnations and/or walk-in opportunities. Oversouls assist souls to investigate potential family situations, physical attributes of the proposed physical body, and expected life experiences based on Oversouls ability to foresee in simultaneous time. Once an incarnation takes place, the Oversoul stays close to the soul and physical body.

Once again, I am amazed at the time frames. The initial Earth was billions of years ago. Souls have been incarnating on Earth for billions of years, as well as incarnating on other planets. I have incarnated on Earth and elsewhere many, many times. My soul is both well-traveled and highly experienced. The same is true of each of you reading these words. Take a few moments to think about this.

Earth's original form as a Christed Planet of Light is once again emphasized by Ea-Ta, as we learn about incarnations taking place on the initial Earth. The presence of Christ Consciousness, from the onset of the planet, is certainly not something that many people recognize. As a premier planet, Earth was set up to broadcast Christ Consciousness to the universe, and then some Creator Gods and physical beings blew it. The planet lost her mission. What a deviation from the Schematic of Source, as the experimenters denied that they required Source's Light.

The idea that Oversouls and their associated souls could pick up, travel to distant planets, and join in the incarnations going on there, shows me the great flexibility of the non-physical realm. Souls are not locked into some sort of a fixed regimentation. This goes along with the whole idea of walk-ins or soul exchanges.

The care given to an incarnation, looking at various potential family situations and other aspects of life in a new physical body is impressive. I can see how seeking the best match for the soul and what it wants to experience in a given lifetime is so important. I see an attitude of caring in the whole process, getting the very best for all concerned. This helps me really appreciate my life in this physical body and all the support I have been given. It helps me appreciate my physical body and all it has given to me in this lifetime.

Discovering that my soul was present long ago, during those early times of Earth's Golden Era, gives me a greater appreciation of just how great is my soul. Since the chances are good that you also were there, think about that in terms of who you really are. Does it give new meaning to your life?

Ea-Ta's communication about receiving my soul when it was handed-off from Andromeda was a real surprise. What a surprise to learn that I had been communicating with my Oversoul.

I am very grateful to my Oversouls who have facilitated my incarnations on Earth, in Andromeda, and elsewhere. They have helped me lead a thousand wonderful lifetimes over the past 10 billion years. What an unbelievable experience! What a trip! Talk about redefining my life ...

Ea-Ta

✶✶✶✶✶✶✶✶✶✶

Subsequent to the above communication from Ea-Ta, questions arose as follows. The first of these concerned an opinion that more than one soul could occupy a physical body at the same time. The answer I received from Ea-Ta was an immediate NO.

The second was the incarnation of dark souls in human bodies. Again, the answer was NO.

Ea-Ta went on to state that, except in the case of a walk-out and a walk-in, a soul, as facilitated by a Planetary Oversoul, is provided at the time of birth. This soul remains with the physical body for its lifetime. Souls are non-physical and are of a much higher consciousness than the physical body they inhabit for a period of time.

At this time, the souls provided to individual physical beings of Earth are charged with a mission to raise the consciousness of the physical body in order to assist the uplifting of the planet. They are to do this within the unique circumstances of their incarnation. This overrides any experiences an individual soul may wish for this lifetime. Whether or not the soul can realize this mission is the challenge of this lifetime.

At this moment, very few humans of Earth understand this mission. Most humans of Earth are focused on having a successful life within the paradigm in which they find themselves.

Many of the problems that occur for humans during a lifetime are related to the rational mind controlling the body, based on the rational mind's goal of keeping the body safe. In addition to this, events, such as disease, can occur with the physical body; these may lead to getting stuck in 3rd Dimension. Then, influences such as childhood trauma, drugs, alcohol, or rape can block the physical body from listening to the urgings of the soul, from striving to higher consciousness. The allures of money and power, along with keeping up with companions who are similarly focused, can lead to actions contrary to the primary mission of the soul.

The implications of Ea-Ta's statement that all souls incarnating on Earth have a mission to raise the consciousness of humanity are vast. There are now 7.6 billion humans on Earth. This means there are 7.6 billion beings whose mission, as dictated by their souls, is to uplift humanity; 7.6 billion unconscious broadcasts ongoing. For me, this is extremely powerful. It leaves no doubt in my mind, despite outward appearances, that humanity is ascending to higher consciousness.

This is true whether the incarnation is for a body to be born into a wealthy and powerful family or the birth is to take place in a refugee camp. It is true whether the incarnation is into a perfectly healthy body or one with serious physical limitations, for a body that will live a long time or a short time. The soul of each is broadcasting. For me, this also explains why souls are eager to incarnate in the physical bodies of the challenged, disadvantaged, homeless, and destitute.

One realization I came to after this communication with Ea-Ta was, that due to all of us having multiple lifetimes, why are we so concerned about dying? Our modern medicine makes a big deal about keeping people alive, at almost any cost. Our laws make it a crime for anyone to commit suicide. Religions frown on suicide. Many books and dramas focus on death. For me, once I came to see my multiple incarnations, death was not such a big thing. It is just the soul deciding to turn in a physical vehicle.

Thank you, Ea-Ta, for your communication, for answering these questions, and for taking good care of my soul.

Blessings,
Mark

Questions about
Ea-Ta's communication:

- Why are the souls incarnating in physical beings of Earth always of high consciousness?

- What is different about souls incarnating on Earth today from the souls who were incarnated during her Golden Era?

- Why do souls incarnate in bodies that are challenged, in difficult circumstances, or will live only a short time?

- Does Ea-Ta's communication cause you to see your soul differently?

Aon

Aon

Aon

I am Aon, the Oversoul who facilitated the Christed Soul of Light that incarnated in the body of Yeshua when he walked on Earth. For billions of years on many, many planets of this universe, my Collective of Unique Oversouls has provided special Christed Souls of Light to create Avatars who are committed to teaching and demonstrating Christ Consciousness during a physical incarnation.

When planetary worlds were created that were not yet by design fully aligned with the Schematic of Source, my Collective of Unique Oversouls was created by Source. Over the billions of years since, my Collective has facilitated the incarnation of special Christed Souls of Light in carefully selected physical beings by means of physical births, light-conceived births, and walk-ins. These special souls have repeatedly reincarnated as Avatars in various physical forms on the billions of inhabited planets of this universe.

We remain close with each special Christed Soul of Light for the duration of its lifetime in physical form to help its physical body demonstrate Christ Consciousness. My Collective also supplies a place for these souls to rest upon completing an incarnation.

My Collective regularly expresses or facilitates many Christed Souls of Light simultaneously and in different locations, such as on different planets. Our special Christed Souls of Light have helped to produce a universe whose trillions of planets and stars are, with very few exceptions, aligned with the Schematic of Source.

In addition to facilitating special Christed Souls of Light for Avatars, we express Souls of Light for incarnations into Exceptional Beings other than Avatars. These incarnations differ from that of an Avatar in that Avatars publicly demonstrate their Christ Consciousness, while Exceptional Beings usually live privately, quietly broadcasting Christ Consciousness. While Avatars may be one in a billion within the populations of a planet, Exceptional

Beings may be more frequent than one in a million. Avatars know who they are and why they have incarnated; Exceptional Beings do not necessarily have that knowing.

Once Exceptional Beings fulfill their initial life mission on a planet, their Souls of Light are handed off to Planetary Oversouls for reincarnation, initially on the same planet. Like all other souls they are then free to incarnate wherever in the universe they wish.

When Avatars retire from repeated incarnations, they become part of the Collective of Ascended Masters, who make their wisdom from incarnations in physical form available to physical beings through messages and energies. It is not necessary for Exceptional Beings and Avatars to be on a planet at the same time.

My Collective of Unique Oversouls is the exclusive facilitator for the incarnation of Christed Souls of Light for Avatars and Exceptional Beings.

In recent times, my collective has focused our attention in this sector of the Milky Way Galaxy. Here there are planets where the Schematic of Source is ignored, where the residents demonstrate little Christ Consciousness. These are the planets of lower consciousness where fear, rigidness, judgment, and domination rule the lives of many. Earth is one of these planets. It is on such planets that we incarnate Souls of Light for both Avatars and Exceptional Beings.

✳✳✳✳✳✳✳✳✳✳

The process of infusing a Christed Soul of Light into the physical body of a being who will become an Avatar or Exceptional being is much more complex than for the incarnation of souls of physical beings who are not foreseen to necessarily become living examples of Christ Consciousness. On a targeted planet, a physical form projected to have potential to become an Avatar or Exceptional Being is singled out by Planetary Creator Gods and Planetary Oversouls. Operating in the non-physical gives Oversouls and

Aon

Creator Gods long-term insights into the projected lives of physical beings in order to make such a determination.

In addition to an above average physical body, my Collective, along with the Christed Soul of Light that is volunteering to incarnate, examines things like projected emotional stability, intelligence, heredity DNA, living situation, physical environment, career, religion, and level of consciousness. This is done to be sure the individual physical being will be able to make an impact, regardless of difficulties that he or she might encounter. We closely examine the proposed family to make sure they will be supportive of this unusual individual.

We look for other physical beings who will be incarnating at the same time to see who among them might become Exceptional Beings to support the activities of an Avatar or other Exceptional Beings.

The activities of my Collective of Unique Oversouls should not be confused with the activities of Planetary Creator Gods or Planetary Oversouls who are charged with the incarnation of the vast majority of physical beings. The souls we express or facilitate only incarnate in unique situations and in unique physical beings of a planet in order to create an Avatar or Exceptional Being who will model Christ Consciousness.

✶✶✶✶✶✶✶✶✶✶

Before the creation of the Milky Way Galaxy, the original Earth was created by Great Beings of Light close to Source. My first experience with Earth was after she had coalesced into a fully Christed planet of 12th Dimension. She then had a resident population of 12th Dimension beings of Light. This magnificent planet acted as an archetype for all other planets in the Milky Way Galaxy. It was foreseen that beings from other planets of the Milky Way Galaxy would visit Earth to see the perfection of Christ

Energy, see Light, Love and Unity at their highest, and return with this to their home planets.

At this time the Galactic Creator Gods were just forming the initial planets of the Milky Way Galaxy. Planetary Creator Gods and Planetary Oversouls would soon populate these with physical beings.

I visited Earth as an individual expression of our collective. I did not manifest a physical form. Rather, I was a non-physical representative of my Collective to experience this magnificent planet first-hand.

What I found on Earth were individual beings living in perfect Love energy while regarding each other with that same energy. With their higher consciousness, they saw me for who I was. I was able to interact with them. I saw Earth as the perfect model of the Christ Energy for which she had been created.

A billion years later, I returned to Earth and witnessed visitors from other planets. By that time, there were many planets in the Milky Way Galaxy; some were at lower levels of consciousness, such as 8th and 9th Dimension. Visitors came from there to Earth to absorb her perfect energies, then returned to their home planets. I was concerned for Earth and her residents because the other planets in the Galaxy were at lower dimensions. However, it soon became apparent that the higher energies of Earth's residents were sufficient to provide the visitors with what they needed of high dimension Christ Energy without being adversely affected by the lower energies of the visitors.

A crystalline grid underpinned the areas of land. Water covered much of the surface of the planet. This was the time of Earth's Golden Era. As she and her physical beings radiated brilliant energy, she set the example of Christ Consciousness for all in the Milky Way Galaxy. Inhabitants of other planets regarded her as a star.

The physical beings of Earth at that time were of 12th Dimension form. Their form was nowhere near as solid as is yours of current Earth. They had no need for food, transportation, clothing, or houses. They were individual forms of color, light, and sound. They were without need for anything because things meant nothing to them.

After my visit to Earth, our Collective of Unique Oversouls supplied a special Christed Soul of Light to an individual of Earth. This was to absorb for our Collective, and the souls we facilitated, how such an ideal planet was functioning. She lived as a being of Light at 12th Dimension, supplying a guiding light to direct visitors from other planets on how to live within perfected Christ Consciousness. Her soul reincarnated repeatedly on the planet. During her time there, she singled out visitors from other planets for whom we later supplied Christed Souls of Light as walk-in Avatars and Exceptional Beings.

The third time I returned to Earth, I discovered a very different situation. The planet was oscillating between 9th and 10th Dimensions. Keep in mind that my Collective had incarnated souls for Avatars on other planets of many dimensions and retained energies from those incarnations. I found the energies from Earth were the same as those experienced on other planets where energies were falling dangerously low.

Our Collective of Unique Oversouls immediately set out to identify suitable physical candidates for Avatars and Exceptional Beings who would demonstrate Christ Consciousness to those on Earth who had lost that connection. We set out to find candidates where the existing souls would walk-out to allow our Souls of Light to enter mature physical bodies.

One such example was Geniva, a young resident of Atlantis who was regarded as someone who could become very spiritual. Her soul was approached with the idea of a soul exchange in order to try and stem the downward spiral of energies by placing the high energy of an Avatar in the population. Her soul agreed and the Christed Soul of Light moved into her physical body.

Aon

For the next two thousand years, Geniva labored to influence those who were acting outside Christ Consciousness. We considered additional Souls of Light, but the consensus was that our involvement would not have a successful result, as the planet continued its downward spiral. The soul of Geniva retired as Earth plunged into 7th Dimension.

✶✶✶✶✶✶✶✶✶✶

Earth then entered a time of dormancy. During that period my Collective focused on placing Souls of Light in physical bodies on other planets. Some planets, in one sector of the Milky Way Galaxy, were functioning at lower dimensions. There were ample opportunities for us to facilitate Souls of Light for Avatars and Exceptional Beings.

Some of these incarnations were successful in raising the energies of these planets. Others assisted planets to retain and boost their coherency with Christ Consciousness. Some of these facilitations were failures, as the Avatars and Exceptional Beings were killed before completing their missions. Unfortunately, these planets of low dimensions continued on their paths of fear, anger, separation, and domination.

✶✶✶✶✶✶✶✶✶✶

Since the introduction of dense physical humans to the 3rd Dimension Earth, 500,000 years ago, my Collective had awaited opportunities to express souls for Avatars or Exceptional Beings who might lift the consciousness of early humans. This went on for many, many years because the minds of your primitive ancestors were such that they could not appreciate the presence of a high consciousness leader or benefit from one who spoke about Light, Love, and Unity, even if it was translated and fashioned to the level of their minds. We had to be very patient during this slow pace of evolution, as we awaited our time to contribute to the uplifting of humanity.

During this time, we assisted Souls of Light to incarnate on other planets. Some of these planets struggled with continued efforts by Creator Gods and physical beings to mesh higher dimension energies and dense physical forms. The physical beings of other planets had dismissed the Schematic of Source, developing civilizations based on fear, separation, and domination. Incarnations on these planets were partially successful in moving some of the residents to higher ways of functioning.

✷✷✷✷✷✷✷✷✷✷

About 100,000 years ago, according to your time, the first opportunity to incarnate a Soul of Light on the new 3rd Dimension Earth presented itself. The humans of that time had advanced to the point that they were collecting themselves into villages. Furthermore, they had now reached a point where they had time to think and contemplate rather than pay attention only to survival. A few of the older members of these communities rose to the status of wise elder. They were regarded by the others as possessing great wisdom accrued from years of life.

It was into the child of one of these wise ones, that we determined to place a Christed Soul of Light, but decided to wait until he was a young man. We regarded the chances of success as better when we could confirm that he had become an independent individual. The child was known as Archamendon; he was born in a town along the Euphrates River by the name of Benefac. It was a town of about 500 people who existed on fish from the river and harvesting of grains and vegetables along its banks.

The child was born without complications, despite his mother's age of thirty years. Her name was Helena. His father's name was Adonite. The family lived in a hut fashioned from mud bricks and a reed roof. Adonite was a fisherman of some renown for he typically caught enough fish to trade with those who had less. You would see their lifestyle as primitive by your standards. Archamendon's early life was defined by his parents, as he assisted them to secure food. By the age of fifteen, he had become an individual but displayed little of anything extraordinary.

This was a foreign concept and was not well received from one so young. Many, particularly the older men, rejected his perspective. However, some of the women came to listen as he spoke about the grandeur of all that was natural and how to be one with it and the non-physical. There were some among the men who resented the attention Archamendon received from the women. They set about to undermine him by killing the animals who visited him.

When this did not stop Archamendon from continuing to speak out, several of the men set upon him one night, beating him severely and telling him to stop preaching nonsense. This did not stop him for long. Although he was crippled, he continued to speak about the non-physical. Eventually his injuries caused his death.

We were saddened by this course of events with our first facilitation of a Soul of Light in a physical human of the new Earth, However, it did not deter us from plans for further facilitations of souls for Avatars and Exceptional Beings. Several of these took place in the ensuing years.

✷✷✷✷✷✷✷✷✷✷

About 2,000 years ago, my Collective was approached by one of our very experienced Christed Souls of Light who wished to incarnate on Earth as a very special Avatar. This soul had become both wise and powerful from successfully infusing Christ Consciousness into physical populations on different planets of this universe over billions of years. This experienced Soul of Light wished to incarnate on Earth in a way that would involve several Avatars and many Exceptional Beings all supporting his plan to introduce Christ Consciousness and make it permanent within the population. This Christed Soul of Light made a powerful argument that it would take a spectacular event to penetrate the stubborn minds and emotions of 3rd Dimension humans. It soon became apparent that this was to be a much more involved incarnation than was our normal undertaking. Thus, we joined in the plan for the proposed physical life of a human of Earth to be known as Yeshua and those to be associated with him.

Our first task was to coordinate the proposed plan with Earth's Planetary Creator Gods and Planetary Oversouls, for they would be providing the majority of the humans present during the time of Yeshua. We foresaw that Palestine would have the right mixture of conventional physical beings, spiritual beliefs, groups competing for power, and a favorable physical location.

In addition to modeling Christ Consciousness, the Christed Soul of Light facilitated for Yeshua wanted to demonstrate to the humans of Earth that death was not the end of their existence, that they would live past death. We foresaw that the Romans would be using torture and death to impose their will on those they wished to subjugate, and we saw a way to use these as part of the demonstration.

The magnitude of what it was proposing was indeed an extensive undertaking. After careful consideration, we saw that it would involve several Avatars and a number of Exceptional Beings to support Yeshua's plan. Due to our status as non-physical beings for whom time does not exist, we were able to see both the eventual outcome and the involvement of many. We could also see the favorable impact of Yeshua's life and the reintroduction of Christ Consciousness.

In coordination with this Soul of Light, we carefully planned the ideal support persons that Yeshua would require to fulfill his mission. Filled with enthusiasm for the project, we set out to construct that support by working backward in the lineage of those to be involved.

Aon

As a starting place we looked for someone to be the patriarch or matriarch of an extensive family. Several candidates were noted. Earth's Planetary Creator Gods and Planetary Oversouls recommended Anna, a woman to be born in Palestine in the near future. It was foreseen that she would live a long time and had the potential to create an extensive lineage. After carefully examining her projected life, we began the search for a Soul of Light among candidates who had successful experiences as Avatars on other planets, who were now available, and who were willing to undertake a very long-term incarnation. It was forecast that Anna could be a mother and grandmother to many who would be supporters of Yeshua. We eventually found a Soul of Light willing to undertake this long-term adventure and facilitated its incarnation into the body of Anna at her birth.

Anna lived for many, many years. She gave birth to numerous children. While she was living out an extended life as a wise leader of the Essenes, she gave birth to a boy who would later be known as Joseph of Arimathea. Foreseeing him as an Avatar to support Yeshua, we facilitated the incarnation of an experienced Soul of Light in Joseph at his birth.

Foreseeing the results of a light-conceived pregnancy and her future lifetime, we facilitated the incarnation of the soul of an Avatar into the daughter of Anna who would become known as Mary, the mother of Yeshua.

Meanwhile Anna's other children were busy giving birth to children for whom Earth's Planetary Oversouls were facilitating souls. For some of these we facilitated Souls of Light to create Exceptional Beings to insure close supporters for Yeshua. In all over one hundred relatives of Yeshua, young and old, male and female, blood relatives and relatives by marriage, would become Exceptional Beings.

Mary of Bethany was the daughter of Joseph of Arimathea. She grew up in an above average household due to Joseph's success in the shipping business. We foresaw that Mary and Yeshua would be attracted to each other at a young age and have a long-term relationship. We facilitated the incarnation of a Christed Soul of Light to create her as an Avatar. Later, we were most pleased when Mary became a powerful influence and a tireless supporter of Yeshua and Christ Consciousness.

The story of Yeshua's life is told, albeit incomplete and somewhat distorted, in the Bible. Later in this book, the Christed Soul of Light that was incarnated in Yeshua will communicate about this.

✳✳✳✳✳✳✳✳✳✳

This physical universe operates almost exclusively according to the same Christ Consciousness that Yeshua brought to Earth. My Collective of Unique Oversouls has focused its efforts for billions of years on achieving that level of acceptance of the Schematic of Source.

The Christ Energy that we have supported through incarnations of Avatars and Exceptional Beings throughout the universe has nothing to do with religion. Religions are a creation of the humans of Earth. The Christ Consciousness we enable is based on unconditional Love and perfect Unity. There is no fear, anger, separation, or domination. It is this ideal that Yeshua brought to Earth.

✳✳✳✳✳✳✳✳✳✳

In more recent times we have facilitated Christed Souls of Light for Avatars into individual humans such as Francis of Assisi, the Dalai Lama, and others for each generation of the humans of Earth. We have also facilitated the incarnations of many Exceptional Beings who live quiet lives in harmony with Christ Consciousness, and then go on to reincarnate many times. It is through these efforts that we are assisting Earth to return to her earlier brilliance as the 12th Dimension planet of her Golden Era.

Aon

Religions have leaders or saints whom they honor or venerate as spiritual examples. Many of them are Avatars and Exceptional Beings who incarnated with our assistance. Most of them did a credible job given their circumstances and the temperament of the people they interacted among. Most taught only a partial understanding of Christ Energy because of their circumstances, and none taught a full understanding of the Schematic of Source. Each did make an impact on the people with whom they interacted.

Some of the religions they founded or supported have fallen into judgment of people who believe differently. Such exclusivity is not consistent with Christ Consciousness, nor is forcing people into a particular belief system. On the other hand, providing the poor and sick with care and Love is very much aligned with it.

It is disappointing to us that there are so few spiritual people who adhere to the perfect Love and unconditional Unity of Christ Consciousness. Nonetheless we will continue to facilitate Avatars and Exceptional Beings on Earth to teach these fundamentals of the universe.

I have enjoyed working with Mark to create this document to inform you of the unique role that Avatars and Exceptional Beings play in the universe. May our words assist you to embrace the fullness of Christ Energy, and help others to understand it.

Blessings,
Aon

MK: "I am Aon, the Oversoul who facilitated the Christed Soul of Light that incarnated in the body of Yeshua when he walked on Earth." These words, coming to me telepathically, really got my attention. My initial reaction was about some sort of an Earth-based oversoul who worked with Yeshua as he incarnated. I had no thoughts of anyone or anything beyond this planet.

After Aon explained who he was, I quickly grasped the implications of the vast revelation about which he spoke. I now see how he opened my mind to receive the vastness of his communication and those of others whose messages are contained herein. This book is the direct result of Aon's communication.

This book has now evolved into a grand vision of the non-physical universe, the workings of Great Oversouls and Creator Gods who create galaxies, stars, planets, physical beings, and Avatars and Exceptional Beings who have influenced the lives of us all.

Thank you, Aon.

✳✳✳✳✳✳✳✳✳✳

As I was awakening to the larger reality, I had read about oversouls, how they functioned with the souls of individuals, and how they were able to help incarnate multiple souls at one time. However, even after nine years of intensive training to achieve higher consciousness, the concept of the Unique Collective of Oversouls, as revealed by Aon, was far beyond anything I could ever imagine.

As I transcribed Aon's words, I came to see that the whole idea of a Collective of Unique Oversouls made a great deal of sense. After all, how do certain people achieve higher consciousness without formal training? How do they come to live in Love and Unity? How do some people rise above the norm for their family, for their race, or for their social-economic situation, to display unconditional spirituality? How do some people become Avatars? How do others become very spiritual in their own way?

The idea of special Souls of Light being incarnated in certain physical bodies makes sense to me. What an ingenious way to set an example for the physical beings of a planet so they might understand the Schematic of Source and see Christ Consciousness, in whatever way their background would allow it to be known.

The extent to which the Collective of Unique Oversouls examined the prospective environment, family, and possible support people for Yeshua led me to wonder just how much thought goes into incarnations of Avatars and Exceptional Beings. It may not be to the extent of Yeshua's, but I am sure much thought is given to each incarnation, in order to fulfill the objectives of the Christed Soul of Light.

I am sure that in many cases, such as with Yeshua, the concepts of Christ Consciousness are hidden in stories to be understood at the level of consciousness of the audience, attuned to the brain power of the populace, and cognizant of their spiritual beliefs. Furthermore, Yeshua demonstrated Christ Consciousness by the way he lived.

✶✶✶✶✶✶✶✶✶✶

Beginning with my 1988 awakening to the reality of inhabited planets beyond Earth, I began to wonder if the Jesus of my Catholic upbringing had gone to each planet and died on a cross. If he was the only Son of God, did the people of these other planets also have to be saved by his crucifixion? Then he must have died a million times. That whole proposition made no sense.

Yet how had these other planets become benevolent, some of them more highly conscious than Earth? Or were they all somehow less than Earth? Could Earth possibly be the most enlightened planet in the universe? I found the latter question almost laughable.

My search continued for thirty years. I learned that the high consciousness light body of Yeshua survived his crucifixion and that his soul was not impacted by it. Yet, according to the Bible, he appeared in physical form to convince his apostles of his resurrection. Once again everything did not make sense.

The disclosure from Aon finally made sense: The soul of Yeshua had incarnated as an Avatar on numerous planets of this universe over billions of years. In each case his incarnation carried Christ Energy to the people of a planet. His many incarnations uplifted the consciousness of the beings of many planets.

✳✳✳✳✳✳✳✳✳✳

The Avatars Anna, Mother Mary, Mary of Bethany, and Joseph of Arimathea were facilitated by Aon's Collective of Unique Oversouls. This placement of souls in relatives of Yeshua was all part of a plan to provide him with a closely-knit support group to help with his mission to bring Christ Consciousness to Earth.

In addition to these souls for the Avatars supporting Yeshua, Aon's Collective also supplied Souls of Light to a large number of Yeshua's relatives who would support him. This too is part of an overall function of this Unique Collective: to supply souls not only of Avatars but also for Exceptional Beings, who quietly exhibit Christ Consciousness in their lives.

I am being told there are many Christed Souls of Light that Aon's Collective of Unique Oversouls has placed in Earth humans since Yeshua.

✳✳✳✳✳✳✳✳✳✳

Aon's description of early Earth gave me further insight into our planet and how special it was and is. Imagine beings of physical form living in unconditional Love and perfect Unity. Imagine what a model it would present for other planets versus the

Aon

3rd Dimension world we currently present. I doubt that the beings from other planets who visit Earth today see it as a beautiful and special place. I doubt that they would take Earth's example home; rather, they now offer to assist us in our resurrection of Earth.

I have very much enjoyed transcribing the words of Aon and learned much.

Thank you, Aon.

Blessings,
Mark

Questions about
Aon's communication:

- What do Avatars and Exceptional Beings have in common?

- What has Aon's Collective of Unique Oversouls achieved?

- Does the existence of Avatars and Exceptional Beings explain how some individual humans excel?

- Does the information from Aon help explain any aspect of your life or that of others whom you know?

Yeshua

Yeshua

Yeshua

I am Yeshua. To be more precise, I am the Christed Soul of Light that incarnated in the body of Yeshua. For ease of communicating hereafter, I will use the name Yeshua rather than referring to me as his soul.

✦✦✦✦✦✦✦✦✦✦

Many billions of years ago, the Special Oversoul Aon expressed my Christed Soul of Light. My Soul's overall purpose was to incarnate in physical form as an Avatar on different planets of this universe.

An Avatar means that the incarnated being is to live and teach Christ Consciousness. To promote understanding of this among the physical beings with whom he or she will be interacting, the incarnation of an Avatar is always tailored to individual circumstances.

The specific reason that my Soul of Light incarnated in my physical body thereby giving birth to me, Yeshua, was to return Christ Energy to Earth. Christ Consciousness had been integrated in all physical beings on the planet during Earth's Golden Era billions of years ago. My Soul entered into my physical body in order to fulfill that mission.

✦✦✦✦✦✦✦✦✦✦

Many years before my birth as Yeshua, my highly evolved Christed Soul of Light came to Aon, with whom it had a long-term relationship. It proposed an unprecedented incarnation to return Christ Consciousness to Earth. Foreseeing the difficult situation into which my soul would be incarnating, Aon recommended assembling other high consciousness beings to support the planned activity of both living according to Christ Consciousness and demonstrating life after death.

To fully implement this plan, both my mother Mary and her mother Anna were incarnated with the souls of Avatars. In addition to Mary and Anna, Anna's son Joseph (of Arimathea) also was incarnated with the soul of an Avatar, as was his daughter Mary of Bethany. High consciousness souls were incarnated in many of my other relatives in order to create Exceptional Beings in my extended family. Such a collection of Avatars and Exceptional Beings had rarely occurred before in this universe.

✶✶✶✶✶✶✶✶✶✶

I was conceived in light energy. My parents, Mary and Joseph, did not have physical intercourse to conceive me. Light energy conception was a process that was practiced among members of the Essene community, a number of whom had been trained to perform it.

My mother, whom you call Mary, was a member of the Essene community. She did not live in one of their cloistered locations, but lived in Nazareth. She had met and married Joseph several years before my birth. My grandmother Anna was a leader of the Essene community.

Essene communities existed in several locations in Palestine and other countries. Generally regarded as a secret sect within the larger Jewish religion, they adhered to a simple lifestyle of diet, meditation, and close family interactions. There were no Priests or Rabbis in Essene communities. Each location existed as a self-contained community with its own buildings and gardens. The Essenes interacted only minimally with the larger Jewish society.

✶✶✶✶✶✶✶✶✶✶

My physical body did not come into your world as described in the Bible. Rather, my birth took place in a small room in Bethlehem. It was at a time of year, April, when there was no snow. My mother Mary was attended by a mid-wife at the birth of my body.

The Bible is correct in that local people learned of my birth and came to visit Mary, Joseph, and me. It is also true that the Magi visited and that we fled to Egypt to avoid the wrath of Herod.

What is not mentioned in the Bible is that my mother Mary, my father Joseph, and I lived in Egypt for a number of years, and that during this time, we were part of an Essene community who were closely allied with the followers of Isis. During this time, we all undertook training to raise our consciousness and experience unconventional ways of seeing life. All the while, we maintained a loose connection to the larger Jewish community.

✶✶✶✶✶✶✶✶✶✶

When we returned to Palestine, I was schooled in the Torah. I did have a Bar Mitzva, as was the custom in that day. This required that I closely study the religion of the Jews and recite many of its teachings.

As a young man, I undertook a series of journeys with members of my extended family. One of these took me to the countries you now call India and Tibet.

There I found wise elders who possessed some of the same abilities and practices as I had seen in Egypt. They practiced meditating to raise the energies of their bodies. I learned how to raise the consciousness of my physical body to a level that nothing of a physical nature would impact it. I learned how to change the substance of material things by converting one substance into another. After several years learning from these wise men, I journeyed back to Palestine carrying the memories of these extraordinary people, the events, and the skills I had learned.

Yeshua

Another time I journeyed to Britain aboard one of my uncle Joseph of Arimathea's ships. He had a fleet that transported tin and iron from Britain to Palestine.

In Britain I interacted with the Druids and saw in them a highly conscious society. With the Druids I lived at a place called Avalon where the Romans had yet to invade. They led me to an enclave of great stones that you now refer to as Stonehenge. There they showed me how they interacted with off-planet beings who descended from the stars. The interactions with the sky beings were very uplifting. All were benevolent.

The Druids were a peaceful culture, but were threatened by the Romans who wished to enslave the populace as workers for their mines, roads, and fortifications, and to appropriate their crops for their soldiers. Here I saw how the energy of domination had infiltrated the Romans. They thought nothing of raiding a Druid village in order to capture the men, rape the women, and leave the children destitute.

I retained lessons from all these visits when I returned to my home among the peaceful Essenes. My grandmother Anna and other members of my family had traveled with me on these voyages, so we had regular conversations to reinforce my impressions and discover how they related to the plan that was now taking form.

Only when I was with Mary of Bethany, my mother Mary, Anna, and Joseph of Arimathea did we discuss that I was an Avatar, as were they. We would each recall our prior lives and some of our incarnations on other planets.

✳✳✳✳✳✳✳✳✳✳

I was married to Mary of Bethany whom you call Mary Magdalene. She was the daughter of Joseph of Arimathea. I had known her since we were children. Ninety-seven members of our very extensive families attended the three-day wedding ceremony at Cana.

It was a very happy occasion; the binding of two people who loved each other very much. It was also the joining of two Avatars who would influence the lives of many physical beings of Earth. This was an important event for us, for our families, and for humanity.

✶✶✶✶✶✶✶✶✶✶

Over her long life, grandmother Anna gave birth to many who in turn birthed many more. We gathered together regularly to enjoy each other's company and to share experiences. Many were Essenes. I was informed that many of my relatives were Exceptional Beings.

At this time, the Jews viewed Essenes as radicals who would not conform to their strict laws and beliefs. In addition, the Romans had conquered Palestine and were governing it in cooperation with the leaders of the Jews. These leaders saw the Essenes as trouble makers. Wishing to support the very tenuous government between the Romans and themselves, they pointed to the Essenes as not in conformity with Roman rule.

This then was the situation as I prepared to begin my teachings among the Jewish people. I had developed a clear model for living and teaching Christ Consciousness in order to bring its Energy back to Earth. My main task was to find words to convey the beauty and scope of Christ Energy to people who were only partially literate and who were steeped in the traditions of the Jewish religion. It was a difficult task because the level of understanding among the Jews rested on the Torah and their interpretation of it by a select group of priests and rabbis. I wished people to see how I was living according to Love and Unity, without adhering to strict Jewish laws, and how it could uplift their lives.

Explaining the Love and Unity of Christ Consciousness to

the leaders of the Jews and changing their minds was an almost impossible task. In contrast, the ordinary people among the Jews were most receptive of my words. I spent many days in silent meditation to achieve the precise wording I used. Some of what I said during that time is correctly contained in the Bible, but the parts pertaining to the larger universe are not.

✳✳✳✳✳✳✳✳✳✳

Dark energy had infected the Jews through the strict laws of their religion and their better-than attitude toward believers of all other religions. Opposition to the perfect Unity of Christ Consciousness is a position that the dark energy has promoted since it emerged during the time of Atlantis. In contrast, I lived and taught peace, Love, and Unity, not judgment or better-than.

The stories about me being opposed by Satan are just that, stories. Satan is a fabrication of 3rd Dimension rational minds who fail to see the subtler aspects of how dark energy infects everyday lives. The attitude of better-than leads individuals to emphasize separation rather than unity. Furthermore, it is easier to blame a distant dark being than it is to look within and take responsibility for oneself and one's actions.

✳✳✳✳✳✳✳✳✳✳

The details of my crucifixion as reported in the Bible are generally accurate. It was my intention to use it and my resurrection to show, in vivid details, that there is life after death. I wished all to remember how I had lived in the high energy of Christ Consciousness, and how I had lived beyond death.

What is not generally known is that the entire event of my

crucifixion was planned well in advance and in great detail, including the participation of my extended family. For example, Judas was a close friend and confident. He reluctantly accepted the task of betraying me in such a way that the Jews and Romans would see my crucifixion to be under their control.

✳✳✳✳✳✳✳✳✳✳

My soul did not depart my battered physical form. My higher dimension consciousness remained strong during all aspects of the torture of my body. During this time in the tomb, I was attended by members of my family such as Anna, Mariam, and Mary of Bethany. They used techniques they had learned in Egypt where resurrection from death was practiced by the followers of Isis. Never did I question my reality as an Avatar, as the incarnation of a Christed Soul of Light.

A few days after I was lowered from the cross, I was able to appear to my followers in the semi-physical form of my etheric body. Most were amazed to see me. Those of a higher consciousness readily accepted me. Those clinging to things physical, could not make the leap to embrace me in my semi-physical state.

My followers, both those of higher consciousness and those in lower, were very disoriented by events. They hid in secret rooms to avoid discovery by the Roman and Jewish authorities. They held meetings to discuss what to do next, now that they had lost my presence. When I appeared to them and encouraged them to remember my life and teaching, some were able to focus on positive future avenues, others were not.

Those who had hoped for a messiah to lead the Jewish people were devastated by my death. In contrast, those who had heard my messages and saw the highly conscious way in which I lived wanted to tell everyone.

Yeshua

Those who were of higher consciousness recalled the uplifting aspects of my life and teachings. Many of them collected small groups where they told and retold the events of my life that had impacted them.

Those who were not of higher consciousness focused on my death and the loss of my leadership. They clung to the words I had said and the miracles I had performed, not the life I had led. They were insecure because they were not grounded by my example.

The Pharisees and Sadducees attacked those who professed to believe my message of Love and Unity. They could not accept that ordinary people could connect directly to God rather than using their intercession as priests and rabbis. These were the same attacks they had made on the Essenes and my followers when I was present. This caused many who believed in me to hide their beliefs.

After a while it became dangerous for many of my family and followers, such as Mary Magdalene and my mother Mary to remain in Palestine. I regularly appeared to them with energies to buoy their spirits and to help them recall my life and teachings.

However, the Jews and Romans continued to pursue them, trying to force them to conform. Thus within a few years after my resurrection, many who had witnessed my life and teachings were scattered. A few remained in Palestine, despite the threat of imprisonment and death. Some went to Egypt. Some fled to countries that you would now call Syria and Turkey. There were also small groups in Britain, France, Greece, and Italy. And a few had gone to India.

I visited with them in these locations for the next forty years. As the years went by, my visits became less in semi-physical form and more in energy manifestations.

I wanted to demonstrate life beyond death in a way people could understand, not so much the resurrection of my body, but the continued life of my soul. That is why I appeared to many in semi-physical form for many years after my death. This was enough for many to grasp that I had survived death and was alive as an example of what was possible for them.

✱✱✱✱✱✱✱✱✱✱

It did not take long after my death for some of my followers to consolidate my teaching in order to form a religion. Some of my disciples wished to have followers, to lead a church, and to leave a legacy.

As I see it now, from my perspective as a non-physical who observed these events, it was much easier for those who wished to create a church to focus on the awful aspects of my crucifixion than on the uplifting energies of my life in a body, to focus on the return of my physical body rather than accepting that a semi-physical perception of me indicated life beyond death. They found success in preaching that people were guilty and that I had died for their sins. Never did I tell Peter to create a church.

They would not allow women into the ranks of their leadership because women challenged the authority provided by traditional paternalism. It was a hold-over from the Jewish religion and other ways of behaving at that time: Men were dominate. Women were subservient.

In all fairness to them, many did try to follow my example of Love and Unity, peace and harmony. But it was a difficult road. And then there were continuing persecutions by both Jews and Romans. This caused many to hide and remain in small groups to support each other. It caused them to be cautious in reaching out to those who had no personal experience with me. Fear was a great deterrent.

In contrast to the efforts to form a church, all that I wished was for people to emulate my life as I walked among them. I demonstrated Christ Energy by accepting all and by loving all as brothers and sisters. I wished my followers to emulate my life, not to focus on my miracles and my death. There is a lesson here for all humanity: Merely live Christ Consciousness. It is not necessary to preach Christ Consciousness.

✶✶✶✶✶✶✶✶✶✶

At an ethereal level, I continued to connect and visit with many who had listened to my message and observed my life. Many of these were members of my extended family. Many were Essenes. Most were former Jews.

I had many long and loving visits with Mary of Bethany to share our love and lay plans to assist others. I also had visits with my mother, Mary. I visited with my apostles and disciples, both men and women, to uplift their spirits and reinforce that I had not died. And I visited with those whom you call the early Christians who had heard my words and observed my life.

When Mary of Bethany and others fled to France and Britain, I visited with them often. I also visited with them when they joined with the Druids to safeguard themselves from the Romans. I enjoyed appearing to them unexpectedly and without fanfare, just joining them as another of their group. I particularly enjoyed interacting with the children who recognized my energy whenever I was nearby.

The main purpose of my resurrection was not physical. Rather, it was to demonstrate that there would be life after death. It was almost impossible to convince some of my followers of anything beyond the physical. Their concept of spiritual was disconnected from the physical, black and white versus integrated. The transition from physical to semi-physical to non-physical levels of consciousness eluded them.

I watched, in sadness, as those who had heard my words and watched as I lived according to Christ Consciousness, were persecuted by both Jews and Romans. The traditional Jews wanted to disprove my message and the life I had led. They also wished to appease the Romans. Some wanted to prove that I was a failed messiah. The Romans wanted only to control the populace. Sometimes they were in league with the Jews, sometimes they persecuted them.

From the beginning of my public appearances, I modified the energy and message of Christ Consciousness to appeal to the people of 2,000 years ago. I interacted with them to reinforce my teachings of peace, harmony, and Love. It was a simple message, but quite different from the judgmental and fear-based environment in which they lived day-to-day. I encouraged them to minister to the needy, the sick, and outcasts, reinforcing that all humans are brothers and sisters.

Much of how I had lived my life in the physical has been lost due to the desire to create a religion. In many respects my early life was quite ordinary except that I had a higher consciousness from birth and was surrounded by highly conscious people. I enjoyed the things that a young boy of that time enjoyed, had friends with whom I played, and adults who cared for me.

There have been many atrocities committed in my name by religions and by religious people. None of these would have happened if there had been no religions and if Christian churches had not insisted on proclaiming me as the Son of God. If those who believed in my teachings had simply followed my example of living with Christ Consciousness and had internalized my messages of Love and Unity, there would have been no religions to dominate others and no atrocities.

Yeshua

As I look at humanity today, I see the majority leading lives consistent with their situation. Just getting along. Most have no larger objective to their lives other than living out their years, knowing they will die.

Religions promise life after death and heaven. They do not speak about lives before this one. Nor do they speak about the opportunities to reincarnate on wondrous worlds of higher dimension or on planets of some distant galaxy. These are all things to look forward to, if you will open your minds.

Few people of this time live according to Christ Consciousness. Most are focused on being comfortable within the paradigm of their situation. A small percentage are lost in 3rd Dimension darkness of fear and separation. They attempt to control others to make their own lives more comfortable. However, life can never be pleasant when fear and separation are at the heart of it. Wealth and power do not change this.

As I taught many years ago, there is life after death. There is a higher way to live in this world. It is not easy to constantly live in peace, harmony, Love, and Unity, but it can be done. It is beautiful and will give great peace to anyone who achieves it.

Furthermore, by doing so, an individual sends energy to others to encourage them to do likewise. The person who functions in Love and Unity influences all about him- or herself, without knowing the effect, because much is at a non-physical level.

I offer the following to my brothers and sisters who are on Earth at this moment. Stand up for Christ Consciousness. See the universe as one with the Schematic of Source.

I say to you, do not be caught in the busyness of modern life. Stay centered in what is important. Live your life without regard to what others think of you. Live in peace, first with yourself. Live in harmony with yourself. Love yourself, then you can love others. See all in unity. See others as your brothers and sisters, and treat them as loving family. For we are all creations of Source and we all are brothers and sisters. I am with you this day. Receive my energy. Know that you are loved.

My Love to all,
Yeshua

MK: Yeshua's communication is so different from what is in the Bible that I would not have been able to comprehend it without the earlier chapters of this book, particularly the one from Aon. *If you have not read these, I encourage you to do so.*

I was very pleased to receive this communication from Yeshua. Parts of it were very emotional for me, possibly due to my memory of a life at that time.

The whole idea that Yeshua and others at that time were Avatars whose souls had incarnated many times before was new for me, something I had never considered. Aon had exposed me to some of this in his communication, but here it was so much more definitive in the lives of Yeshua, mother Mary, his grandmother Anna, Mary of Bethany, and Joseph of Arimathea.

His communication is very direct, explaining that he came to Earth to demonstrate Christ Consciousness by living it.

Of importance were the revelations about the Essene community and the key roles its members and his extended family played. With their close association and simple lifestyle, I can see why this particular group of individuals was chosen as the cast in the drama that Yeshua planned.

That Aon's Special Collective of Oversouls had incarnated

Yeshua

Exceptional Beings within Yeshua's relatives explains how a large contingent of people were available to support Yeshua's plan. I suspect many of these are reincarnated at this time.

Then there was the plan that the soul of Yeshua put in place around his death and resurrection. Aon and he went to great lengths to insure there was a supporting cast for the drama that was to unfold. It was all so well thought out, including his training in Egypt and Tibet.

Yeshua's conception in light energy reinforced the virgin birth, but more importantly it shows that it was practiced among the Essenes and Egyptians. His mother Mary was also light-conceived.

Then there was the birth of Yeshua at a time of year when the weather was pleasant, in a room attended by a mid-wife, not a manger.

Yeshua's travels to India, Tibet, and Britain filled in the years that the Bible ignores. In Tibet he spent years learning some of what he would later demonstrate. In Britain he interacted with Druids —whom I had previously considered to be ignorant savages— and where he interacted with extraterrestrials. Although he never mentioned it publicly (or did he?), these encounters must have been important to the way in which he conducted his life. I can see how his travels and insights from wise people conflicted with the Catholic view that he is the only Son of God and as such is all powerful.

Yeshua's marriage to Mary of Bethany had a special significance for me as I had previously visualized Mary as described in the Bible. Yes, there were books and movies, like the DaVinci Code that opened the whole subject of her relationship to Jesus. However, Yeshua's description of their marriage produced an emotional reaction in me.

Yeshua

Stepping back from the descriptions in the Bible, and seeing things by way of the eyes of the soul of Yeshua, I now better understand the roles that the Romans and Jews played. The Romans were the conquerors of Palestine, treating it much like any other conquered territory. For them it was just another occupation in a long series of conquests. They needed to control the conquered population, putting it to work to support their needs. Sometimes this required a demonstration of their power (i.e. crucifixions). As is common with any conquest, they made agreements with the leaders of the people to assist them. It is not much different today with conquering powers.

The dark energies had infected the Jews of Palestine, causing them to live in fear of a wrathful God, while feeling better-than, as the chosen people of that God. They viewed people like the Essenes as less-than those who lived by their strict code. This then was the 3rd Dimension stage upon which Yeshua chose to carry out his plan.

After his resurrection, Yeshua visited with many people in the semi-physical form of higher consciousness. From my perspective I would equate this to 7th Dimension or higher, where physicality gives way to the semi-physical, yet there is enough of the physical remaining to indicate form. I can well imagine that people who are used to totally physical existence would find it very difficult to accept a fuzzy image as the real thing. I too have found it difficult to explain the semi-physical and the non-physical to people.

I had not realized that Peter was so intent on forming a church almost immediately after Yeshua's resurrection. I had read about the Council of Nicaea in 325 and thought that was the start of the organized Catholic church. But Yeshua tells us that the push to form a standardized belief started almost immediately after his death. I believe it was founded on the example of the Jewish religion and its structure. I think it was also a function of Peter wishing to act as a powerful intermediary with God and head-up the organization. The exclusion of women from Peter's church has continued to this day.

The push to focus on Yeshua's crucifixion and humanity's guilt lent a power of attraction to the organization of the early church. This was in direct opposition to the life of Yeshua, that demonstrated the unconditional Love and perfect Unity of Christ Consciousness. I believe I can see the influences of dark energy and ego versus Yeshua's example of peace, acceptance, and Love.

Through his life, his words, and his resurrection, Yeshua has had a significant impact on this world. Despite its many faults and misdeeds, and its dogmatic approach to other beliefs, the Christian religion has helped to feed the poor and homeless, establish hospitals, and provide schools. Christians fall short of unconditional Love and perfect Unity, but in many ways, they are better than those who are totally under sway of the dark energies of fear, separation, and domination.

I was surprised to learn of the shipping between Britain and Palestine, and the extensive travel to distant countries by people of Yeshua's time. I was also surprised to learn of the connection between the Essenes of Egypt and the followers of Isis.

I see the lifestyle of the Essenes as quite advanced in that they were self-sufficient communities, were closely connected to the spiritual without any dogma, and functioned close to their families.

This communication from Yeshua helped me to recognize the one-eighty degree turn I had made, when I had turned my back on Jesus and the salvation scenario of Catholicism. I now have made a three-sixty since I understand what Yeshua's life was really all about. Now with this communication, and what I have learned in other communications from him, I appreciate fully the message of Yeshua's life and embrace the Christ Consciousness he delivered. As I was typing Yeshua's words, I felt an energy of closeness to him.

Along my path of searching out a spirituality with which I could be comfortable, I encountered several opinions about the crucifixion. Among them were that he felt nothing because he was of such high frequency. Then there were those who denied that it had ever happened, and those that said it happened in the 3rd Dimension but it affected nothing beyond that. I now see that the body of Yeshua did indeed suffer, but that his higher self remained focused on who he really was.

The concept of Jesus as the Son of God, his only begotten son, was finalized at the Council of Nicaea in 325 A.D. It had been preached by some prior to that time, but had not become dogma. By naming him the Son of God, it gave the Catholic church a charter that it was better than all other religions. This led to atrocities in the name of Jesus.

In the early church there was much confusion about Jesus and what he had said and done. Many different stories circulated. Some people pointed to his lifestyle. Some focused on his miracles. Some wanted a church, some did not. The push to form a religion with a single dogma was promoted by Peter and Paul as they sought to convert the gentiles. Those who recalled the life of Jesus were pushed aside as the power of the organization asserted itself. Yeshua tells us he never gave Peter a mandate to form a church.

I particularly resonated with Yeshua's final words. I am trying very hard to see all of humanity as my brothers and sisters, as well as all in the universe. As I typed the words of this communication I felt very close to Yeshua and felt his energy.

Thank you, Yeshua.

Blessings,
Mark

Questions about
Yeshua's communication:

- Why did Yeshua's Christed Soul of Light incarnate on Earth?

- Who were the other Avatars supporting Yeshua's mission?

- How did Yeshua model Christ Consciousness?

- What was Yeshua's relationship to the Essenes?

- How does Yeshua's communication change your views about the life of Jesus?

Mary of Bethany

Mary of Bethany

Mary of Bethany

I am Mary of Bethany. I communicate with you today as the Christed Soul of Light that was incarnated in Mary's physical body 2,000 years ago. You probably recognize the name *Mary Magdalene*; it was the name attributed to my physical person by later Christians. Those who knew my physical manifestation at the time of my life on Earth knew me as Mary of Bethany.

Let me begin by pointing out that during that lifetime in my physical body I was part of the Essene community in what is now called Israel. There were other Essene communities in Egypt and other countries around the Mediterranean. Essene communities were tightly knit groups that followed strict rules of diet and behavior, lived in quiet seclusion, and embraced a direct connection to the non-physical. The Essene diet consisted of vegetables, fruit, eggs, milk and bread. We were self-sufficient communities growing all our own food. There was little disease due to our healthy diet. As travelers, we were always welcomed into other communities of Essenes where we were provided with food and shelter.

Essenes were considered to be a minor sect of the Jews. While we adhered to many of the teachings of the Torah and celebrated the Jewish holidays, our beliefs were much more wide-ranging than strict Jewish dogma and laws. We mingled little with the larger Jewish society, preferring our seclusion.

Within our secret communities we knew about and awaited the coming of a Great Being of Light. We saw him as an inspiration; we did not see him as a savior or a ruler.

✹✹✹✹✹✹✹✹✹✹

My father was Joseph of Arimathea. He operated a fleet of ships that transported tin, iron, and other ore from what today you

Mary of Bethany

call England to Palestine. Because of my father's status as a wealthy ship owner, my upbringing was quite pleasant.

I found pleasure in the things that young girls of that day enjoyed: friends, discoveries, games, and family. I also enjoyed interacting with boys as we explored the countryside. I had red hair and was told that I had a joyous disposition. My mother was Mary of Magdala.

I was raised in my father's wealthy household near Jerusalem. Our family participated with the Essenes, but did not live in one of their communities. Because of his success in business, my father was accepted as one of the elites of the Jewish community.

On one occasion, when we went to visit my grandmother Anna in one of the Essene communities, I met Yeshua. Even at our young age, he and I were immediately attracted to each other. We knew that we were Avatars and felt the energy of each other. We knew we were different, but it would be several years before we knew what that fully meant.

For the rest of my life in the physical body, I was known as Mary of Bethany. I was never a harlot. That characterization was the result of the paternalistic Christian church that emerged after Yeshua's lifetime. It was promoted by men who were jealous of my relationship with Yeshua, denied our marriage at Cana, and wished to dismiss women as equal to men. The name Mary Magdalene was applied to me when I was characterized as a harlot.

At an early age, I traveled to Egypt with members of my extended family. There we lived in an Essene community for several years, receiving training from members of the ancient sect of the goddess Isis. It was there I learned of light-conceived pregnancy and practiced life extension rituals. I also watched initiates give up their bodies and then return to them, rising from the dead.

Mary of Bethany

Long before Yeshua began his public ministry, I fell very much in love with him, knew exactly who he was, and foresaw what his life was to be. I foresaw my life with him and knew we would be married.

Yeshua traveled to India, and was gone for several years. I did not accompany him on this trip. It was then I knew that I truly loved him and should be at his side always. When he returned we made plans to become one.

Later as young adults, we traveled with groups of relatives to Egypt, India, and Britain. Like others in the group, I was dressed in a long robe with a belt about my middle and sandals on my feet. To care for our bodies, we bathed often and rested along the way during our long treks.

Along the way we always found food and shelter with friendly families. Others in the group had made these trips before and knew the way. Never did we feel threatened or discouraged.

Each trek took months to complete and we remained at our destinations for several years. There we enjoyed the company of happy, enlightened people who shared what they had and what they knew.

✶✶✶✶✶✶✶✶✶✶

Yeshua and I were joined as husband and wife in the marriage ceremony in Cana. This wedding was ours, the joining of two Avatars. It was attended by members of our Essene communities and by our many relatives. The three-day celebration consisted of stories, dancing, and food. The Bible incorrectly characterizes this as the wedding of others.

From that moment I was always at Yeshua's side, as he went about his teaching mission. I watched as he put Christ Consciousness into words that ordinary people could understand, and as he demonstrated Christ Consciousness by living it. I was there when he performed miracles and healed people.

Mary of Bethany

Each place we visited Yeshua attracted a crowd who was eager to hear his words. In each crowd there were as many women as men. I found great pleasure in interacting with the women who saw me as an adjunct to Yeshua. As before, we were always welcomed into homes and supplied with food.

Early in our relationship, Yeshua explained to me his plans to die and then be resurrected. He went about gathering people around him who would support this idea. Many were close relatives. The purpose of this was to show people that there was life after death and that the body was merely a vehicle for an eternal soul of vast proportions and power.

In the years following our marriage, I traveled with Yeshua to Turkey and Egypt. Everywhere he went, his energy drew a crowd of interested people, particularly children. He always taught and demonstrated a life of Christ Consciousness of peace, harmony, Light, Love, and Unity. All of this occurred before he began his public life in Palestine. People were happy to hear his alternative to the traditional religion of the Jews.

✱✱✱✱✱✱✱✱✱✱

Yeshua's crucifixion was carefully scripted with our relatives, male and female. Each fulfilled his or her particular role. I watched the torment of his body. I accompanied his body to the cave where we who were knowledgeable ministered to it, as we had been taught in Egypt. Soon his etheric body emerged from the badly damaged physical body.

✱✱✱✱✱✱✱✱✱✱

After the crucifixion and Yeshua's resurrection, Yeshua and I were able to spend time together as a married couple, but never did we engage in physical intercourse. I gave birth to three light-conceived children.

Mary of Bethany

Because the traditional Jews feared the message of Yeshua and his energy of Christ Consciousness, and because the Romans wished to control us along with the Jews, we were forced to abandon our traditional Essene communities in Palestine. A group of us journeyed to Egypt seeking a place free from Roman and Jewish threats. By that time, almost all of the Essene communities had embraced the teachings of Yeshua. Although they had somewhat different interpretations of his teaching, the focus on his life was consistent.

The persecutions by both Jews and Romans continued. After a while, our Essene community in Egypt was no longer able to shield us. The Jews saw us as troublemakers and wished to stamp out the messages taught by Yeshua and the example of his lifestyle. The Romans merely sought to control all under their domination.

In the company of others, I fled to the south of France where a small Essene community had been established free from Roman domination. Other followers of Yeshua were now scattered about the Mediterranean.

✱✱✱✱✱✱✱✱✱✱

It was during this time that some of the followers of Yeshua began to focus on creating a church. This effort, driven by Peter and Paul, was somewhat successful despite persecutions by the Romans. Those who were part of the Essene communities were greatly disturbed by what they perceived as a distortion of Yeshua's teachings and the example of his life. Yeshua never intended to create a church. His was a simple message of peace, harmony, unconditional Love, and perfect Unity to be practiced by individuals who would connect directly to Source without a priest or minister.

Along with the drive to create a church was a total disregard for the contributions of women. This despite the fact that women had comprised an equal number with men among the followers of Yeshua. This served to isolate the Essene communities and me from other followers of Yeshua's teachings.

When I attempted to enter into discussions with the leaders of this church, telling them that Yeshua never intended such, I was dismissed. I told them that Yeshua wished all to focus on his life and messages, not on his miracles and death, and that people could communicate with Source directly without the need of an intermediary.

✶✶✶✶✶✶✶✶✶✶

I gave birth to our three children while in France. I remained there for a time, caring for them. After they reached an age that the rest of the Essene community typically oversaw their education and upbringing, I resumed my visits, first to nearby towns.

Everywhere I traveled and with all groups I met, I was honored as the spouse of Yeshua. In many instances Yeshua was with me, in his etheric form. Always did I speak about the value of women, bring their contribution up to that of men. Always did I encourage all to administer to the sick and needy..

I lived for many years at the Essene community in southern France. I also traveled to Britain and Turkey, interacting there with communities of Essenes and other followers of Yeshua's teachings. Some of this travel was with the semi-physical Yeshua. I eventually assumed the role of wise elder who consistently delivered a message of Christ Consciousness.

When I was incarnated on Earth, Yeshua and I worked very hard to maintain the purity of his message and life. We were most disappointed when it was subverted by the egos of a few men. After many years of teaching and interacting with people, I left my physical body at the age of seventy.

I am most pleased to add to the efforts to return Earth to her former position as a 12th Dimension planet of Light, and encourage all to discover the truth about Christ Consciousness and to live it each day.

I give my love to all on Earth.

Blessings,
Mary

✶✶✶✶✶✶✶✶✶✶

✶✶✶✶✶✶✶✶✶✶

MK: I was very pleased when Mary Magdalene contacted me and I feel privileged to have had this message from her. This is the first time she had communicated with me. Knowing other versions of who she was, I am most happy to have her tell her true story.

Each Great Being of Light who has communicated with me for this book has projected a different energy. The energy of the Soul of Mary of Bethany is pure enthusiasm. She was excited to present her message.

✶✶✶✶✶✶✶✶✶✶

Her communication explains much about her life. It is quite different from what is generally accepted by traditional Christians, quite a different story than in the Bible. I particularly appreciated her revelations about who she really was as a young woman, her relationship to Yeshua, and her status as an Avatar. I now see how she was such a valuable support for Yeshua.

Her relationship to Yeshua has been alluded to in books and movies, but here it is very clear. They were married. They had children. She supported Yeshua's mission throughout her life in a physical body, and taught many, particularly after moving to France and then traveling to other countries.

I was surprised at the time she spent in Egypt learning from the followers of Isis. I was happy to see her reaffirm her life in France, as it has been referred to by others.

I find it significant that there were as many women as men among those who followed Yeshua's teachings, and that Peter and Paul excluded women from any significant role. This has carried on to the present-day Catholic church.

I believe that placing women in secondary roles has created many of the current-day problems in this world. I believe women play a critical role in restoring Earth to its former glory as a 12th Dimension planet.

So, I ask myself, "What were the male followers of Yeshua so afraid of? Why did they need to reject the contribution of women?" One can attribute their attitude towards women to the traditional ways of the Jews and other societies of that time. But was that it, or were there other reasons?

I see dark energy infecting Yeshua's followers as they ignored the way in which he lived and some of what he taught. It seems to have influenced some to pick and choose among his actions to support their desired dogma, and to marginalize women because women pointed out the truth of Yeshua's life and teachings. What the Catholic church went on to become is far from Yeshua's message of unconditional Love and perfect Unity. Yeshua taught his followers to communicate directly with God without the need for a priest as an intermediary.

With Mary Magdalene, I see a beautiful example of how an Avatar influenced people with whom she came into contact, while at the same time leading the normal life of a physical being.

Thank you, Mary. It has been my pleasure to communicate with you.

Blessings,
Mark

Questions about
Mary of Bethany's communication:

- What were Mary's interactions with the Essene community?

- Why was the marriage celebration at Cana important to Mary?

- What did Mary do after the resurrection of Yeshua?

- What was Yeshua's relationship to the Essenes?

- Does Mary's communication change how you view Mary Magdalene?

Master Kuthumi

Master Kuthumi

Master Kuthumi

I am Master Kuthumi, of the Realm of Ascended Masters. We are the Collective of Christed Souls of Light who have incarnated as Avatars in physical bodies on Earth and on many other planets. We offer the lessons of lifetimes in physical bodies, such as you now possess, because we have lived in them.

I communicate today on behalf of all in my Collective. We interact with the physical beings of Earth to support the resurrection of all to 12th Dimension.

The way in which we Ascended Masters work with you is much like your experiences with Archangels and other great Beings of Light. We are happy to communicate with you when asked. Ascended Masters bring intense energy to you, uplifting you, offering you insights, coaching you, and informing you of ways to lift your own energy.

✴✴✴✴✴✴✴✴✴✴

Most humans of Earth are of the 4th Dimension; fear does not rule their daily lives, but it is always in the background. They go about their lives fluctuating between feelings of love and anger, hoping for the best, accepting what comes along. Most do not focus on the non-physical, other than to attend church once a week.

At one extreme of the spectrum of Earth's humanity are those who embrace 3rd Dimension where fear, separation, and domination rule their lives every moment. Some seek to accumulate power and wealth, and to dominate others to achieve their ends. Others cower in victimization, despair, poverty, homelessness, or addiction.

At the other extreme are individuals of 5th Dimension

consciousness who embrace Love and Unity in its many manifestations. Without necessarily knowing, or openly professing the details of Christ Energy, they see spirituality as the foundation of their lives and live accordingly.

★★*★*★*★*★

The institutions of your modern civilization have all been infected by dark energy. These include: Governments that exist for the wellbeing of those in power, not for the populace they govern. Legal structures are slanted toward those with money and power versus those without. Monetary systems are structured around the accumulation of wealth in the hands of a few. Many not-for-profit institutions now focus on monetary aspects versus focusing on the services they once provided. Most religions preach love, but do not practice it unconditionally, as they judge others as less-than. Wars are fought over these different perspectives.

The media generally supports the ruling class by emphasizing the ills of society, not its uplifting aspects. Burning of fossil fuels continues despite its impact on the environment. Damage to land, water, and air is ignored in favor of providing a comfortable lifestyle. The plight of the lowest levels of society, the poor, the homeless, immigrants, and the victims of war are ignored in the name of preserving what the wealthy consider to be their entitlement. Racial discrimination is practiced in most societies.

From one perspective, much of your modern civilization resembles that of Atlantis in its final days with dark energy controlling its path to self-destruction.

However, there are several important differences compared to Atlantis. The population of Earth is widely dispersed, particularly in terms of its perspectives. There are an important few who are dedicated to achieving an enlightened lifestyle though they may not understand all of the reasons behind their actions or the larger picture of ascension to 12th Dimension.

There is the active participation of Archangels and Ascended Masters, like ourselves. There are the beings of inner Earth who assert themselves in support of Earth's resurrection. And finally, there are extraterrestrials who prevent beings of dark energy from entering the planet, focus beneficial energies to all on the planet, and display their craft to heighten awareness. Such was never the case with Atlantis.

These external supports make a huge difference. Like physicians treating a cancer, they are shining light on humans who would pursue 3rd Dimension ways of fear, separation, judgment, and domination. This light has a healing affect much like x-rays destroy cancer. With their non-physical light, they surgically remove humans who embrace the ways of dark energy as their misdeeds are shown to all. We foresee that the combined efforts of humans and non-humans will result in an ascended Earth.

✶✶✶✶✶✶✶✶✶

We Ascended Masters are particularly dedicated to uplifting the humans of earth so that they will hold the energy of higher consciousness. In line with that we offer the following:

- We encourage each individual to *honor and maintain his or her body*. It is much easier for a healthy body to embrace the energies of higher consciousness. We encourage both healthy diet and exercise.

- *Find quiet time each day* so you are separated from the busyness of day-to-day life. Taking time each day will enable you to project quiet competence. This will reduce the effects of the dark energy as it seeks to deflect you from maintaining a lifestyle based on Love and Unity.

Master Kuthumi

- *Choose a path to spirituality that resonates with your heart.* It is okay to explore several paths, but settle on one for a time and absorb all that it has to offer. Then move on if you are called to another path.

- *Recognize that your physical body is an instrument of your soul,* in which it seeks to gain experiences. Think of your body as a vehicle and allow your soul to drive it.

- See your soul as a Great Being of Light that has existed for a very long time. *Know that you have had many incarnations and will have many more.*

- Discover why your soul came into this body at this particular time. *Focus your life on your soul's mission.* Put to one side the attractions of living in the 3rd Dimension world. Focus on what makes you happy without being diverted by the conventional paradigm.

- *Discover your chakras* and how working with them can raise the consciousness of your physical body as well as your non-physical bodies.

- *Find a stability with money.* Do not let it control your life. Set realistic goals that will maintain you first and foremost as one with Christ Consciousness.

- *Set an intention to lead a balanced life,* one that accommodates day-to-day life, but has as its goal something higher than merely living out your days on Earth.

- *Find ways to connect with efforts to resurrect humanity and Earth* and lend your energy to them.

- *Seek out people who reflect your values* rather than people with whom you merely spend time. Engage in deep conversations.

- *Find opportunities to be of service to your brothers and sisters.* Devote time to serving others.

- *Enjoy the beauty of your wondrous planet.* Take long walks in nature or on a beach.

- *Find balance in your life between the spiritual and the physical.* Seek to live in the spiritual, not just pay lip service to it. Make it a focal point of your life.

- You are on Earth at a critical time. *Know that you came here for a reason.* Find that reason.

- Earth is undergoing change. There are even greater changes coming. *Live your core values,* so that you can rely on them as change comes into your life.

✳✳✳✳✳✳✳✳✳✳

Your soul, Mark, was expressed during the initial creation of souls for 12th Dimension Earth. As such, it is of very high consciousness. This is likewise true of those with whom you feel a close connection.

Since it was first manifested 10 billion years ago, your soul has had a thousand lifetimes, on Earth and on other planets of the universe. You have also had extended periods when your soul rested with a Planetary Oversoul.

Think about the vast number of experiences your soul has accumulated during these many lifetimes. Some of these have been in beautiful high consciousness worlds of light, some in dark worlds at your choosing. Often your soul incarnated into physical beings who developed into teachers, wayshowers, philosophers, and healers. In every case, your soul accumulated experiences that now makes it very wise.

Think about what your soul has learned from a single lifetime such as you are now undertaking. Multiply that by a thousand, then consider the accumulated wisdom. It is almost beyond comprehension, is it not?

This current lifetime has been a difficult one. Yet, you have made the transition from a 3rd Dimension upbringing to now operating in the 5th Dimension. Your story is not unlike that of others. Think this when you relate to another person.

✶✶✶✶✶✶✶✶✶✶

As has been explained in other sections of this book, the dark energy is real. If allowed, it can invade the energy field of an individual, infecting it like a cancer.

A physical body rejects cancer cells all the time. They make no impact, otherwise a physical body would succumb to the very first cancer cell to enter it. Likewise, a healthy being of high consciousness can reject dark energies so they have no impact. This happens all the time, otherwise the entire population of the world would have succumbed to dark energies.

The attitude and consciousness of each individual enables him or her to accept or reject dark energy. Even those who have had a traumatic experience can reject its influence. The same holds true when you experience momentary anger or depression. Recognize it as such, then return to higher consciousness. In the same way that an alcoholic or drug addict can overcome an addiction, so can you overcome the influence of dark energies. It may not be easy, but it can be done. Many turn their lives around after difficulties.

It is the energy of the individual that determines the outcome of a silent invasion of cancer into the physical body. It is the attitude of an individual that determines how they will respond to a subtle attack by the dark energies.

Do not blame the dark energy for how you are living. It is up to you to decide how you will live. Like doctors treating cancer patients, so we of the Ascended Master Realm stand ready to provide energy of Love, Light, and Unity to anyone who requests it. And like a cancer patient, the desire of the patient is all important. If you desire to live at high consciousness you will find ways to do so.

****

As you have been informed earlier in this book, the physical human body today is the result of many years and many influences. It has much evolved from its beginning 500,000 years ago.

Surrounding the physical body is the etheric body. Next comes the mental body, followed by the emotional body and the causal body. The spiritual lies beyond these four bodies. Each of these bodies surrounds the physical body, like layers of an onion. Each of them has important functions.

The etheric body contains the seven principle chakras associated with your physical body. Beginning at the lowest, they are the root chakra, the sacral chakra, the solar plexus chakra, the heart chakra, the throat chakra, the 3rd eye chakra, and the crown chakra. Each of these play important roles in the functioning of the human body. There are twenty-one principle chakras, the other fourteen exist above the head. There are also many other chakras associated with the physical body.

As an individual progresses toward higher consciousness, the functioning of these non-physical bodies and chakras will be upgraded from the way in which they functioned at lower consciousness. *Discover how these affect your life.*

To achieve functioning at the 5th Dimension, a person needs to control his or her thoughts, emotions, words, and action at every moment. They will need to integrate unconditional Love and perfect Unity. When an individual achieves this level of function, they will know and feel high consciousness.

When they slip out of this high level of functioning, they fall into 4th Dimension, where fear and other energies may impact them temporarily. At 5th Dimension there are no energies of fear, separation, or domination.

✽✽✽✽✽✽✽✽✽✽

Mark, you asked me to give you a meditation for inclusion in this book. Please use the following:

Picture yourself in a field of yellow and red wildflowers. The sky is a beautiful blue with wispy white clouds. Walk through this field to a small hill on your left. There you will find an opening in the hillside. Walk through that doorway.

Inside is a large cavern. It is very quiet within and brightly lighted in a soft glow of pink. Proceed to the center of the cavern to a table upon which burns a magenta flame.

This is the flame of Source. It is always available to you here and in your sacred heart. It is pure Love from the All That Is. Know that you are a reflection of this light in physical form.

Take a seat near the table. You see other physical beings seated around you. Some appear to be human, others are much different. Know that all who are seated here are your brothers and sisters, though they may appear strange to you, though they may be from some other planet. You are all children of Source.

On the sides of the cave are living plants. They are vivid green and lush with flowers of many colors. Their scent fills the space with a delightful odor. You feel completely at home, knowing that you are one with this manifestation of Source. This is the feeling of perfect Unity. Know that you are one with all in the cave from the brilliant light of Source to the other physical beings to the trees and flowers. Know that you are love and that you are loved. Relax into this knowingness ... ...

After a while you rise from your chair and exit the cavern. Walk back into the wildflowers and blue sky. Walk down a gentle hill to a path. Turn to the right.

Other people are walking on this path. Most pay no particular attention to you, but you know that they are aware of your energy. A few turn as you pass, they nod or smile, but they do not speak to you. You are aware that you are broadcasting your energy for all.

You recognize that you can return to the cave whenever you wish to reinforce your uplifting energy. You are confident that you are uplifting others without speaking to them.

✶✶✶✶✶✶✶✶✶✶

Your task, if you choose to embrace it, is to discover who you really are: A great soul with many lifetimes of experience incarnated in the physical body of a human of Earth. Once you understand this, you will undoubtedly love yourself. Once you love yourself, then you can love others. This is the energy that a highly conscious individual transmits to others.

Master Kuthumi

Then you can go the next step and embrace Christ Consciousness, Love and Unity. Then you will see all in Unity as expressions of Source. Then it will be quite easy to love all regardless of their color, race, behaviors, or beliefs. The key to this is to focus your energy so that you transmit who you really are. People will recognize you at an unconscious level regardless of your physical appearance.

So, what can you do about the situation of humanity at this moment? All that you need do is to live your life at the highest you can achieve, whatever that means to you. Live in unconditional Love and Perfect Unity. Your powerful uplifting energies will help transform humanity and the Earth.

Each human on Earth is incarnated with a soul that knows its mission is to assist the evolution of Earth to higher consciousness. This includes those existing in poverty as well as those existing in plenty. It includes those who have succumbed to the infection of dark energies as well as those who are living in the Light. All souls come with the same mission.

What is not usually understood is that each person, regardless of their environment or socio-economic condition, has this mission. They may be in difficult circumstances, but what they make of it during this lifetime is all important. It may seem inconsequential to you, but, in the larger scheme of things it is all important, for if one individual fails to live in the Light, then all of humanity is impacted.

It is most important for those living in higher consciousness to be aware of that everyone is doing the best they are able, given their attitude and circumstances. Everyone is functioning to the best of their abilities given the body, and mental and emotional capabilities that they have. Each is your brother or sister. In another lifetime, the child in a refugee camp, or a homeless person on the street, may have been your father, mother, sister, or brother. See each human in this way. Value each human in this way. Know that each human is a valued expression of Source. Know that each has a beautiful soul that is not too different than yours. See in this way. Love one another in this way.

It has been my pleasure to communicate with you.

Blessings,
Kuthumi

✶✶✶✶✶✶✶✶✶✶
✶✶✶✶✶✶✶✶✶✶

MK:　I was most pleased to receive this communication and meditation from Master Kuthumi. I had listened to his messages in other situations, but had not previously received messages directly from him.

I found the meditation most helpful as I was typing it. Then reading it again, I see the impact of understanding that we do influence those arounds us, at the very least, unconsciously.

Master Kuthumi's comments on the dark energy lend emphasis to the fact that it is energy, not some super power that has risen up in opposition to Source. Nonetheless, it is a powerful energy that works in subtle ways to influence the lives of all except those who live according to Love and Unity.

Master Kuthumi's words about the situation on our planet resembling the final days of Atlantis struck a chord with me. I can see the comparison in the way that many segments of our society behave in self-centered ways. I also know that there are groups of people around the world dedicated to assisting the resurrection of Earth. In other chapters of this book, we see how we are being assisted by beings from inner-Earth, by off-planet beings, and by Archangels. I have been told that the outcome this time will be

Master Kuthumi

much different than was the case in Atlantis.

His reference to how we should see others, no matter their current incarnation, really struck home, particularly in light of the troubling issues with immigrants. I now see those that are homeless, addicted, or immigrants as my brothers and sisters, as possibly my relatives in past lives or future ones. What a refreshing way to embrace all in Unity.

Thank you, Master Kuthumi.

Blessings,
Mark

Questions about
Master Kuthumi's communication:

- Which of Master Kuthumi's recommendations do you find most important?

- Think about the experiences your soul has accumulated over its many lifetimes.

- Does Master Kuthumi's communication assist you in living at higher consciousness?

Archangel Michael

Archangel Michael

Archangel Michael

It is I, Archangel Michael. My realm of Archangels and Overseers of the universe was expressed by Source at the onset of this universe. We have been supervisors of and participants in all aspects of it for billions of years.

I am personally acquainted with the physical and non-physical beings who have contributed their messages as recorded in this book.

The Words in this book that were ascribed to individual beings are truly their words, as recorded by Mark. Each of the Great Beings of Light is real, as are the physical beings; make no mistake about that. Mark's words are accurate recordings of the messages that each of these beings conveyed to him. Additionally, as Metatron said in his opening remarks, the words in this book carry an energy.

Mark's comments after the communications of these Great Beings are his words. I generally agree with them, but not so for every comment.

All who have supplied communications for this book are pleased with our participation in this important document.

✶✶✶✶✶✶✶✶✶✶

The communication from Zi-An is indeed from a Creator God of the Milky Way Galaxy. His recount of the way in which that Galaxy was formed, the individual stars, and the planets thereof, is consistent with my observations of the process involved and its results. The core of the Milky Way Galaxy is still active today with new stars being born in order to recycle older ones.

Archangel Michael

The communication from Zi-An about the creation of Earth is most important. It is vital that the human beings of Earth understand that the planet on which they live was once the most brilliant and majestic planet in the Milky Way Galaxy. It was a model of Christ Consciousness for other planets. The Adam Kadman beings who lived on Earth at that time were of high consciousness. They demonstrated living in oneness with each other, loving all, and being in unity with their environment.

It is this result on which we Archangels are focused as we help to raise the consciousness of all on Earth. We wish to restore Earth to its Golden Era as a planet completely in line with the Schematic of Source.

I believe you will find Zi-An's statement about positioning the 3rd Dimension new Earth in its current orbit most interesting.

✦✦✦✦✦✦✦✦✦✦

The communication from Actin, one of many Creator Gods of Earth, is of importance to the humans of Earth today because it helps you realize who you really are: descendants of a very long lineage. Yes, your body is your physical expression, but it is important to realize that you have ancestors from 500,000 years ago. It is also important to know that your ancestors were lovingly created with great expectations. Humanity has evolved a long way since this onset.

Of equal importance is Actin's description of the care taken to nurture the new Earth of 3rd Dimension, to make it habitable for humans. Earth today retains much of her original beauty, but much has been lost due to humanity's desire to conquer her, rather than living in harmony with her. Actin actively cooperates with other Great Beings of Light to assist in raising the energy of Earth at this time.

Archangel Michael

Actin commented on the beneficial activities of beings from other star systems and how they had helped humanity with their DNA and interactions. You are humans of Earth. You are also children of the universe. Think of this as you look at the many different expressions of the humans of Earth today.

It is entirely possible to have many of the features of a modern civilization without raping the land, without polluting the air and water. As humanity's consciousness grows, it will move in this direction. The longer it takes to return to oneness with Earth, the greater will be the struggle to return her to her previous status as an extraordinary example of creation.

Please pay close attention to the words of Actin about Earth's Golden Era. This is the model to which we are restoring the planet upon which you live. 12th Dimension Earth was quite different from 3rd Dimension Earth.

✶✶✶✶✶✶✶✶✶✶

Adama's communication is of importance first because it discloses the existence of beings living in inner Earth. This alone may give you pause, as it disrupts conventional ways of seeing who shares your planet.

The beings of Telos are actively supporting the ascension of humanity by contributing their energies to the evolvement of the physical bodies of humans. They are not that different from humans and have a desire to share.

Of secondary importance is the disclosure that the current civilization of Telos began 25,000 years ago. Furthermore, that this recent civilization is based on a civilization of Earth's Golden Era, billions of years earlier. There is no direct physical connection to that earlier civilization of Lemuria, but there is the connection held by the imprinting of the souls present in Lemuria long, long ago. This demonstrates the power of souls as they determine their incarnations and the longevity of their existence.

✶✶✶✶✶✶✶✶✶✶

The message from Adrial discloses that other parts of the universe are not necessarily like Earth or the Milky Way Galaxy. The star-planets of Andromeda show quite clearly that there is much more in this universe than has been imagined by the rational minds of the humans of Earth. Beings at 15th Dimension are quite different from the humans of Earth. It should open your minds to the possibilities within the Schematic of Source.

There are implications for Earth in Adrial's message: Higher consciousness brings higher temperatures for a planet and her physical beings.

The communication from Adrial also demonstrates the fluidity of souls as they pass from one incarnation to the next. A soul can be at one level of consciousness during one incarnation, while at a very different level the next.

Justine's communication shows a very human-like relationship to Mark, despite their current differences in levels of consciousness. Connections like this abound as souls incarnate time and again with friends and family.

✶✶✶✶✶✶✶✶✶✶

The communications from the Beings of the Pleiades and Sirius show how we Archangels have flexibility to be where we are needed. The Archangels of these two constellations have assisted the physical beings to maintain their connections to Christ Consciousness despite attacks by dark energies. The fact that they have maintained their connection to Christ Consciousness over billions of years gives a glimpse of its majesty and its great power throughout the entire universe. It also shows how the influence of dark energy can be thwarted, by maintaining the high consciousness of Christ Energy.

That entire planetary systems have existed in this way for billions of years should give all on Earth a vision of what is possible, what you can achieve on your planet. Beings from both constellations have interacted with humans of Earth in supportive ways. This shows the benevolent attitude of most extraterrestrials and their attachment to the humans of Earth.

I believe you will find the comments about whales and dolphins insightful, for they hold positive energy for your planet. They contribute much to your ascension to higher consciousness. That they were introduced from another planet brings into focus the limitations of science, as the rational minds of scientists dismiss extraterrestrials and the influence of the non-physical.

✳✳✳✳✳✳✳✳✳✳

Ea-Ta communicates a very different picture about incarnations of souls in bodies than is commonly accepted. Oversouls are actively involved in these incarnations, whether into a new born baby or a walk-in into an older human body. Planetary Oversouls are the leading edge of the vast non-physical beings who orchestrate this universe. They are the ones who enable the spiritual to be connected to the bodies of human beings.

Note the care that is given to each incarnation. This care is the same whether it is an incarnation into the body of a royal baby or the baby of the poorest resident of a slum. It matters not whether the child is white or black, male or female, intelligent or challenged, or whether the person is to have a grand career on Earth or is to be quite ordinary. Oversouls take great care in facilitating the incarnation of the soul of every human being of Earth. Each soul has a plan for each incarnation. Oversouls go to great lengths to help a soul accomplish its plan.

Ea-Ta's statement that all souls incarnated on earth have a mission to raise the consciousness of humanity has vast implications. That means that there are over seven billion physical beings with that mission, as dictated by their souls. With that vast accumulation of energies, let there be no doubt, despite outward appearances, that humanity is ascending to higher consciousness.

✦✦✦✦✦✦✦✦✦✦

The communication from Aon is in sharp contrast to that from Ea-Ta. Aon's Collective of Special Oversouls deals with Christed Souls of Light who are destined to be incarnated in the bodies of Avatars and Exceptional Beings. These are the one in a million or a billion who will fully dedicate their lives to living in Christ Consciousness and demonstrating it to others.

Avatars and Exceptional Beings are in sharp contrast to the more usual incarnations of souls who have lifetime after lifetime seeking experiences to advance their goals. Many souls incarnated in physical bodies live far from Christ Consciousness for a lifetime. Some intentionally live a dark life to learn what they do not wish.

Aon has been at work since the earliest days of the creation of this universe. His Collective has facilitated millions of incarnations. These incarnations have resulted in a universe that is 99.999% aligned with the Schematic of Source. These activities have resulted in Christ Consciousness spreading throughout the universe.

Archangel Michael

Aon communicated about the soul of Yeshua coming to his Collective with a plan for his life on Earth. Five Avatars and many Exceptional Beings were facilitated to support Yeshua's ambitious plan. Several incarnations were into light-infused pregnancies.

✶✶✶✶✶✶✶✶✶✶

The soul of Yeshua communicated about aspects of his life as a human of Earth that are not found in the Bible. As a young man, he traveled to India and Britain, and learned much from contact with people there. He recounts his pleasant experiences as a member of the Essene community of Palestine. These revelations are not spoken of in the Bible for they do not conform to Christian dogma about Jesus as the only son of God.

Yeshua communicates how his crucifixion and resurrection were carefully planned, three generations in advance, with the members of his extended family. Again, very different from what is written in the Bible.

Yeshua tells us about his marriage to Mary of Bethany at the marriage ceremony at Cana. A different story from what is presented in the Bible.

Yeshua speaks about his life after his resurrection and how he remained on Earth for many years, supporting those who believed in his teachings. He speaks about his time with Mary and how they taught together in various countries.

Yeshua shows his disappointment at the way in which his life and message have been contorted. He does not comment on his later anointment, by the Christian religion, as the only son of God, and the center of that religion.

In later discussions with him, I found him to be most disappointed with that turn of events, for now people worship him. Worship places the worshiper in a place of less-than. When one recalls who they really are, they see the situation differently.

The soul who came to Earth as Yeshua has continued to incarnate as an Avatar in physical bodies around the universe. None of these have been as challenging as his lifetime on Earth.

✶✶✶✶✶✶✶✶✶✶

Mary Magdalene communicated in order to set the record straight versus how she is portrayed in the Bible. I think she did that very clearly.

She and Yeshua were very much in love. They found ways to complement each other as they went about teaching. It is not disclosed in the Bible that she was a very powerful teacher, appealing to people in ways different than Yeshua. As a couple, they made an excellent team that helped many Jewish people accept what Yeshua was saying. After his resurrection, they continued to teach as a couple.

Mary's life of service as an Avatar should be celebrated for she lived according to Christ Consciousness, demonstrating it to assist many to see a better life.

✶✶✶✶✶✶✶✶✶✶

The Soul Master Kuthumi has had many lifetimes on Earth, so it speaks from many accumulated experiences. It is dedicated to assisting humanity to raise its vibration so that all might enjoy a more blessed life, free of fear and all that comes with it.

I am very pleased that he enumerated the many things that each person can do to move themselves along the path to higher consciousness.

Archangel Michael

I would add only this: Focus on discovering who you really are. When you truly know this, you will be able to love yourself. Once you love yourself, you will be able to love everyone else.

✶✶✶✶✶✶✶✶✶✶

It has been my pleasure to have worked with Mark to create this book. I have been with him every step of its writing. Within its pages are disclosures never before made public. Use this material to help know who you really are in a universe sense and as expression of the Divine.

Each word of this writing, be it from a Great Being or from Mark, carries with it energies that are beneficial to you. Absorb what you can from these words, then pursue living as one with Christ Consciousness.

✶✶✶✶✶✶✶✶✶✶

Let me suggest a few final thoughts:
The next time you look in the mirror, recognize that you are the physical vehicle of a great soul that has incarnated a thousand times. What do you believe that your soul might have learned?

When next you view someone about to transition from his or her body, celebrate with them knowing, your soul will likely encounter their soul in the future. What does this tell you about your own life in physical form?

TThe next time you look at the night sky and see the many stars, recall the words of Zi-An and how he was involved in creating the Milky Way galaxy. How does this change your opinion about the universe? How does it change your opinion about God?

Next time you take an airline flight across an ocean, recognize how far it seems. Now think about how far it is to the closest star. Can you even begin to conceive of the vastness of the universe? Can you see how vast is Source, the All That Is?

Recall that Earth was once the most extraordinary planet in the Galaxy, a 12th Dimension model for all. Know that you are here to assist the return of humanity and Earth to 12th Dimension. How does this change how you view your life here?

The next time you look at a human being who is struggling with life on this planet, recall that the soul of that person may very well have incarnated as your father, mother, brother, or sister. How does that change your opinion of that person? Can you now begin to comprehend perfect Unity?

Blessings,
Michael

Transcriber's Notes

This book has been the most exciting and rewarding project in which I have ever engaged. It was first suggested by a communication from Aon, then grew as more Great Beings communicated their messages.

This book is not my composition, rather it is the words of Great Beings of Light that I have recorded as they have communicated them to me. I am humbled to have been the transcriber for their words.

There are many ways to see the complexity and vastness of the universe and the myriad beings who populate it. I offer the words of this book, the communications from Great Beings of Light, as one such way.

I am told that one reason for this book is to anchor the concepts and information coming from these non-human sources into the Earth plane. The results of this are words that carry energy. Allow that energy to settle within you as you read the words. I know that I feel them as I write.

I am very grateful to Archangel Michael, for he has been with me throughout the writing of this book, encouraging me and offering advice.

My earlier books were based on lower levels of consciousness, beginning with the extraterrestrial phenomenon. When I was asked to post communications from Justine, a non-human, at my web site, my consciousness took a major leap upward. The communications in this book had to wait until I was of a high enough consciousness to fully grasp their wonders and record them in English. It required that I grasp who I really am in the larger picture to fully comprehend what I received.

Embracing the information in this book will help you comprehend who you really are in a universe sense, understand the wonderful soul that inhabits your body, and find higher consciousness. Then you will be able to unconditionally Love yourself. Then, and only then, will you begin to understand the reason why you incarnated at this time and in this place. When you connect to this, you can appreciate perfect Unity with the All That Is. At the very least, this book will change your opinion about God, death, and life on Earth.

And perhaps you too will glimpse through the words of Ea-Ta and Archangel Michael that your soul incarnated here to assist humanity to ascend to higher consciousness.

Blessings,
Mark

Mark Kimmel

Mark has spoken at international forums, been a guest on radio and television shows, and has conducted workshops based on his unique insights into the transformation of Earth and his interactions with non-physical beings. Mark's earlier books are *Trillion, Decimal, One, Birthing A New Civilization, Transformation, Chrysalis, Icebreakers,* and *Cosmic Paradigm.*

Aon, Voices of the Nonphysicals is an altogether new adventure for Mark in that it features channeled communications from 15 non-humans on subjects ranging from the creation of the universe to who we, the humans of Earth, really are and what is our destiny.

By focusing on non-physical beings in his writing and speaking, Mark weaves a credible picture of the larger reality while presenting an uplifting vision for the future of humanity and of our planet. He presents his communications with Archangels and other nonphysicals without a religious orientation.

Mark's passion for writing and teaching about non-physicals is far different than his earlier career as a successful businessman, where he worked for major corporations and founded and ran three of the most respected Colorado venture capital funds. He retired from business in 1996. Mark has been listed in *Who's Who* since 1985. He has degrees in engineering, marketing, finance, psychology, and divinity.

Mark is married with two grown sons and five grandchildren. He spends his days writing and speaking about this, the pivotal juncture in human history, and how each person has the power to impact all on this planet by living at higher consciousness. He is the founder of the Cosmic Paradigm Network, an international group dedicated to manifesting Earth's transformation.

CONTACT for Mark Kimmel

Email: CP@zqyx.org
Web Site: http://www.cosmicparadigm.com/